E242
EDUCATION: A SECOND-LEVEL COURSE

LEARNING FOR ALL

UNIT 11/12
HAPPY
MEMORIES

Prepared for the course team by
Tony Booth

The Open
University

E242 COURSE READERS

There are two course readers associated with E242; they are:
BOOTH, T., SWANN, W., MASTERTON, M. and POTTS, P. (eds) (1992) *Learning for All 1: curricula for diversity in education,* London, Routledge (**Reader 1**).

BOOTH, T., SWANN, W., MASTERTON, M. and POTTS, P. (eds) (1992) *Learning for All 2: policies for diversity in education,* London, Routledge (**Reader 2**).

TELEVISION PROGRAMMES AND AUDIO-CASSETTES

There are eight TV programmes and three audio-cassettes associated with E242. They are closely integrated into the unit texts and there are no separate TV or cassette notes. However, further information about them may be obtained by writing to Open University Educational Enterprises Ltd, 12 Cofferidge Close, Stony Stratford, Milton Keynes MK11 1BY.

AUTHOR'S ACKNOWLEDGEMENT

I would like to acknowledge the work Felicity Armstrong put into the early development of Section 4 of this unit, on truancy, and for her help in gathering information on exclusions. I also owe thanks to the teachers and education welfare officer who contributed their time and information.

Cover illustration shows a detail from 'Midsummer Common' by Dorothy Bordass.

The Open University, Walton Hall, Milton Keynes MK7 6AA

First published 1992. Reprinted 1994

Edited, designed and typeset by The Open University

Printed in Scotland by Thomson Litho Ltd, East Kilbride

ISBN 0 7492 6112 9

This unit forms part of an Open University course; the complete list of units is printed at the end of this book. If you have not enrolled on the course and would like to buy this or other Open University material, please write to Open University Educational Enterprises Ltd, 12 Cofferidge Close, Stony Stratford MK11 1BY, United Kingdom. If you wish to enquire about enrolling as an Open University student, please write to the Admissions Office, The Open University, PO Box 48, Walton Hall, Milton Keynes MK7 6AB, United Kingdom.

CONTENTS

1 INTRODUCTION

1.1   This unit is about conflict in education. Conflicts in school and the lessons we derive from them may provide the most powerful experiences and memories of our schooldays. For many teachers and students, a concern with conflict and control takes precedence over learning and the resolution of difficulties in learning. How can students begin to learn if they do not attend to what is being taught or do not turn up for school? Yet we argue, in this course, that the temptation to give priority to matters of control should be resisted. For how can we expect students to give us their attention if we create inappropriate and insufficiently engaging curricula?

1.2   In the next brief section, Section 2, 'Conflict in school', I will ask about the nature of school authority and disaffection. I will consider how disaffection is rooted in the way students are valued in school and focus on a group of young women in 'bother'. I will argue that there is a culture of conflict between students and teachers which may prove remarkably resistant to change.

1.3   In Section 3, 'Weeding out', I will examine the variety of responses to students who are seen to be difficult or 'challenging' in their behaviour. I will explore how students come to be categorized in the statementing process as having emotional and behavioural difficulties. I will look, too, at the exclusion of students from school and attempt to account for the rise in exclusion rates in the early 1990s. In particular I will examine the disproportionate exclusion of black students from Afro-Caribbean backgrounds which occurs in many local education authorities.

1.4   Section 4 is about students that opt out through truancy. I will look at how truancy can be defined, at the numbers involved, the characteristics of students who truant and the reasons they and others give for their absence. I will consider the variety of responses to truancy from government, educational welfare officers and others.

1.5   In Section 5, 'Abusing power', I will look at the excesses and abuses of power between students, between teachers and students and between schoolworkers themselves. While bullying is usually seen as a problem that affects school students, I will argue that it is also commonplace between adults and between adults and children. Further, I will suggest that efforts at curbing it will have limited success until its roots in the adult world are exposed. I will ask whether sexual and racial harassment, sexism and racism should be seen as forms of bullying and will look at the attempts in one school to challenge sexist stereotypes. I will end the section, controversially for some, by looking at the abolition of corporal punishment in state schools, and the reactions to and implications of the abolition.

1.6   Section 6, 'Stemming the tide: providing support?', is about attempts to reduce the categorization of students as difficult or challenging in their behaviour. It examines a behaviour support service, established from the resources released by closure of a special school for students categorized as having emotional and behavioural difficulties. I then compare this service with the description of the variety of activities engaged in by 'behaviour support teachers' in another local education authority in England. Finally, I look at the different policy climate in the Lothian region of Scotland.

HOW SHOULD THIS UNIT BE STUDIED?

1.7   This unit is expected to take four weeks. Section 2 is relatively short. Sections 4 and 5 are the longest sections, though Section 4 has no additional reading. In addition to the unit text, you will be required to work on the following chapters, audio-cassette and television programmes:

Section 2 Conflicts in school

Reader 1, Chapter 19: 'Lassies of Leith talk about bother' by Gwynedd Lloyd.

Section 3 Weeding out

Reader 2, Chapter 29: 'Settling the score: responses to young deviants' by Mel Lloyd- Smith.

Reader 2, Chapter 16: 'On being a client: conflicting perspectives on assessment' by Derrick Armstrong and David Galloway.

Section 4 Opting out: truanting from school

No additional readings.

Section 5 Abuses of power.

Reader 1, Chapter 20: 'Bullying in two English comprehensive schools' by Colin Yates and Peter Smith.

TV6 *Danger, Children at Play.*

Reader 2, Chapter 6: 'Challenging patriarchal culture through equal opportunities: an action research study in a primary school' by Sheila Cunnison.

Cassette 2, Programme 3: 'Memories of corporal punishment'.

Section 6 Stemming the tide: providing support?

Reader 2, Chapter 33: 'Challenging behaviour support' by Paul Howard.

Appendix 2 'Themes and variations in behaviour support' by Bob Sproson.

Section 7 Investigations

No additional readings.

CONFLICTS IN SCHOOL

On top of old smokey,
All covered with sand,
I shot my headmaster,
With a green elastic band.

I fired him with missiles,
I fired him with pies,
I could not have missed him,
He was forty-foot wide.

I went to his funeral,
I went to his grave,
Some people threw flowers,
So I threw a grenade.

I came to conclusion
He wasn't quite dead,
So I took a bazooka,
and blew off his head.

(Playground song, Cambridge)

2.1   This song was sung with great relish by a group of primary school children who, while not angelic, were relatively conforming in school. They accepted the value of 'learning' but in conforming to the school culture they also accepted the ideology of opposition to teachers: all teachers are inhuman until proven otherwise. Singing about the violent death of their headteacher gave them great pleasure. It was part of the same repertoire as their stories about how his assemblies were repeated with little variation to each new intake of children. Are such violent fantasies children's innocuous retaliation against those who hold power over them? Or do they reveal the tip of a culture which needs to be changed if levels of disruption and disaffection in schools and exclusions from schools are to be reduced?

2.2   The 1986 Education Act in England and Wales requires headteachers to instil into the students in their care 'a proper regard for authority'. The interesting feature about such a statement is not its presence in legislation but that it is there without explanation. For those framing the Act, who should be recognized as having authority as well as how citizens should respond to it was unproblematic. Yet what is a proper regard for authority in a democracy? Who should be in authority and how should it be exercised? When is authority legitimately used and when is it abused? Is there a proper *disregard* for authority?

2.3   I discussed the interaction between authority, disaffection and devaluation in the introduction to *Producing and Reducing Disaffection* and the issues are reflected in many of the chapters of that book (Booth and Coulby, 1987). Authority relationships in school are not separate from relationships outside it. They depend on a structure of dominance in society. Some people and some categories of people are more powerful than others. Their positions are sustained by a vision of normality in which a particular hierarchy of power relationships is represented as ordinary life. This normality may be enforced by those willing to take on positions of authority. The nature of such positions may be obscured by the double meaning of the word 'authority' which implies greater knowledge as well as more power. An authority is the person who 'knows best'. This confusion of meaning may mislead both those who aspire to and those who are subjected to authority. It is a familiar enough occurrence, which has potential for both humour and intense irritation, that when someone changes their power position they may not only swagger and strut but also believe that they are the sudden recipients of wisdom. Those in authority also obscure the powers they serve by representing 'obedience to authority' as morally desirable and criticism of current power relationships as an abnormality, an 'authority problem'.

2.4   Many teachers are well aware of the structural determinants of their power, as one secondary teacher remarked: 'Moving up the hierarchy counts for an awful lot and the title of head or deputy head brings respect and credibility.' A primary headteacher was alarmed, at first, by the extent of the power her position conferred as well as the wisdom she was expected to display:

> When I became a head I was terrified by how much power you have. People are prepared to give you limitless power. At first it was awful here as the staff were forever asking if they could do things rather than just getting on with it ...

> Even the parents view me as some sort of referee. Recently two mothers were fighting outside in the playground. They came into school for me to judge who was right and who was wrong.

2.5   In requiring headteachers to instil 'a proper regard for authority' into students, the 1986 Act recognized the position of teachers in maintaining existing power structures. Teachers may support existing power relationships and adopt the mantle of authority with pride, literally if they wear a gown. Alternatively they may attempt to subvert them. In any case, they will usually discover that part of the complexity of understanding their own authority is that their power is embodied in the teaching profession in a diffuse and precarious way. There is no gown-clad silhouette within the system, tailored perfectly to their own shape, which merges with their body and instantly confers unquestioned deference. Such a merging of person and structure may seem to be achieved in a few public schools where history gives each occupant of the head's office a pope-like infallibility. But for most teachers, while the battle may be weighted in their favour, their authority still has to be fought for. Once it is gained, it may be maintained by threat of coercion or the subtle illusion that when their wishes prevail 'all is right with the world'. This illusion may foster a delusion of grandeur, in which a challenge to the teacher comes to be seen as a personal affront. But if the authority of schooling does not reside within the bodies and minds of individual teachers but has political origins then the challenge to authority is not simply a personal matter.

2.6   The explanation of conflicts in school, then, is complex. Conflicts arise through structural and cultural as well as personal relationships. Students *can* be troubled and they can also be inconsiderate, unkind and aggressive. The purpose of this brief section and the unit as a whole is to enable us to raise questions about the 'natural order' of power relationships in school and to stand back from the urgency of classroom conflict. Besides developing more appropriate and flexible curricula for the diversity of students, can we create a code of conduct for all the participants in education which reduces the likelihood of opposition and confrontation?

WHAT IS DISAFFECTION?

2.7   Disaffection in school, as elsewhere, is a feeling of opposition. Among school students, it is a rejection of the teacher or of what is taught or of the methods of teaching and learning or of other aspects of the school. Because it is a sense of dissatisfaction with what is offered in school, it will always affect the quality of the experience of school and may also reduce a student's attainments. Of course, feelings are often mixed. Many students, and many teachers, reject some aspects of school life without this having a dramatic effect on their performance in school. But we should try to reduce disaffection for these students as well as for those whose opposition radically reduces their achievements.

2.8   Disaffection is a common feeling and it may come and go. No doubt some of you will have been irritated by the content or approach taken at various points in this course. But unlike students in school you have the freedom to leave the course or to concentrate on the parts that you like most or to supplement the material we provide with other reading. It is far harder for students in school to take this mature attitude to learning.

2.9   Some of you may experience feelings of disaffection only very rarely. Others may find that such feelings are more common, at home or at work, or at play, as a learner or as a teacher. What situations produce disaffection in you and how do you cope with feelings of rebellion?

Disaffection and devaluation

2.10   Some groups of people in our society are valued less than others. Many people suffer a sense of devaluation based on their class or occupation or skin colour or sex or sexual orientation or abilities, attainments, disabilities or appearance. These processes occur outside and inside schools and have been referred to at several points in this course. They will be looked at again at a number of points in this unit, particularly in Sections 3 and 5.

A captive audience?

2.11 If you are devalued you are likely to become disaffected when this becomes apparent to you. Whether or not this leads to rebellion, as well as the form that any rebellion takes, may depend on a number of factors. Rebellion may spill out in an apparently irrational and uncontrolled form, it may be avoided because of a recognition of the difficulties in changing the *status quo* or because of temporary lack of support or because those in authority have effective means of control. In *Producing and Reducing Disaffection* (Booth and Coulby, 1987), I drew attention to a story by Nawal El Saadawi (1975) which traces the connection between sexual oppression and one woman's violent response.

> With each of the men I ever knew, I was always overcome by a strong desire to lift my arm up over my head and bring my hand smashing down on his face. Yet because I was afraid I was never able to lift my hand. Fear made me see this movement as being something very difficult to carry out. I did not know how to get rid of this fear, until the moment when I raised my hand for the first time. The movement of my hand upwards and then downwards destroyed my fear … the movement of my hand had become very easy, and everything in my hand could be moved with a natural ease even if it were a sharp knife which I thrust into a chest and then withdrew … I am speaking the truth now without any difficulty … When I killed I did it with truth and not with a knife … That is why they are afraid and in a hurry to execute me. They do not fear my knife. It is my truth which frightens them.
>
> (El Saadawi, 1975, p. 102)

I include this as a graphic reminder that even where systematic devaluation does not lead to disruption the potential remains there simmering.

PERSPECTIVES ON BOTHER

2.12 You may recall from Unit 1/2 that in the case study on the Grove a teacher found herself talking about the difficulties of instilling middle-class values about education to children who come from working-class backgrounds. She corrected herself, realizing that there was something amiss with her complaint, that her perception about the lack of interest of the pupils might be inaccurate or that perhaps it was up to her to make the classroom compatible with the pupils' cultures. However, it is likely that she was expressing her feelings about a clash of culture between herself and some of her students. Some teachers have had less hesitation about wishing to instil a new culture in their pupils. One teacher spoke to me about the way she liked to make her nursery class 'an extension of home', but it was clear that she was not referring to a home extension for the pupils:

> Most of our homes are not how I would want a home to be. But when a child's been three years in the home you're not going to say

immediately 'you're wrong, your mother is wrong, don't do it like that'… his self-image will fall, he'll get two conflicting standards, but if we can gradually ask him to conform to our standards rather than immediately …

(Nursery school teacher, personal communication)

This teacher seemed to think it is both desirable and possible to detach students from the culture of their homes. The change may seem feasible at the nursery stage when the gap in size and sense of power between teacher and pupils is so great. As students get older the cultures and subcultures of students reassert themselves. Can schools provide a home base for all of them?

Activity 1   Talking about bother

Now read 'Lassies of Leith talk about bother' by Gwynedd Lloyd, which is Chapter 19 in Reader 1. In it a group of girls discuss disruption and getting into trouble in school. Their discussion ranges over many of the issues I will raise again in later sections of this unit. As you read it think about the following issues.

- How would you feel about teaching this group of girls?

- Do you learn anything from this group of Scottish girls about what they want from teachers and their experience of school?

- Do any of the complaints they make appear legitimate to you?

- Would the information in this article help the teachers of these young people to work more successfully with them?

- Do the young people have a perspective on education that is inevitably antithetical to the values of schools? Could the school develop a culture in which these girls feel comfortable?

- How do you feel about this style of gathering information?

2.13   What these young women say sparks off all sorts of thoughts in me about the nature and value of schooling. They do not indicate a clear single perspective on school life. They portray a school subculture in which opposition to school and 'winding up' of teachers are essential components. A teacher is commended because 'he could see it from your point of view' (p. 219) but if teachers were simply to adopt the perspective of these students, they too would be in opposition to school. The girls do not portray themselves as considerate or respectful of the feelings of others. They mock the speech of a teacher and are happy to see a teacher cry. It is not just teachers whom they see as on the opposite side of the fence, for when parents choose between support for them or for school authority, they usually come down on the side of the teachers.

2.14   However, I find some of the arguments about the ownership of space in school persuasive. The girls try to define a territory for themselves in school and seem to see the toilets as an area to make their own. They try to customize the schools' clothes, although in Scotland schools cannot compel students to wear school uniform. They feel uncomfortable about menstruation and do not see their teachers as making sufficient effort to put them at ease about it. This is the clearest claim that the school is not set up as a place where girls can be as equally at home as boys. Could schools do more to allow these young people to be themselves in school without diluting expectations for respectful behaviour and educational progress?

2.15   One of the main lessons I would try to take back into the classroom after reading about the views of these students is that the opinions of members of the group differ about the value of education and much else besides. It is a mistake to create a uniform stereotype about any group.

2.16   However, I think I would remain cynical about the possibilities of removing opposition altogether. As the authors of a study on discipline in schools remark:

> We suggest that a variety of pupil sub-cultures would continue to exist whatever the overt and hidden curriculum. As long as schools mean teachers in authority over pupils some degree of disaffection and disruption seems inevitable. The extent of such disaffection and disruption in a new Jerusalem of curriculum and assessment can only be a matter of speculation.
>
> (Johnstone and Munn, 1987, p. 27)

3   WEEDING OUT

3.1   In this section I examine the variety of responses to students who are seen to be difficult or 'challenging' in their behaviour. I will explore how students come to be categorized in the statementing process as having emotional and behavioural difficulties. I will look, too, at the exclusion of students from school and attempt to account for the rise in exclusion rates in the early 1990s. In particular I will examine the disproportionate exclusion of black students from Afro-Caribbean backgrounds which occurs in many local education authorities and examine the reasons for it.

3.2   The first part of this section relies heavily on two chapters in Reader 2.

Activity 2   Categorizing for care or control?

In 'Settling the score: responding to young deviants', Chapter 29 in Reader 2, Mel Lloyd-Smith provides an overview of the provision made for young people who get into trouble at school or through the courts. In order to absorb the chapter you will need to broaden your focus from education to include all areas where challenges to authority and law can occur. Mel Lloyd-Smith asks us to examine our motives for intervention in all such cases. In all contexts he sees the response to the 'deviance' of young people as primarily concerned with control rather than care.

Mel Lloyd-Smith discusses the situation in England and Wales rather than Scotland and Northern Ireland. Trends differ in these places and this needs to be born in mind, particularly if you are a student in either place. Gwynedd Lloyd has gathered together a very useful collection of articles about provision in Scotland which continue Mel Lloyd-Smith's themes, called *Chosen With Care? Responding to disturbing and disruptive behaviour* (Lloyd, 1992).

The chapter contains a mass of facts and figures and it may need to be chewed over slowly for these to be digested. As you read the chapter consider the following issues:

- What do you think of the possibility, raised in section 1 of the chapter, that 'the expansion of provision for deviant youngsters has itself contributed to the increased incidence of deviance'?

- What explanations are given for the growth in educational provision for children and young people categorized as disruptive or as having emotional and behavioural difficulties?

- What influence is the 1988 Education Act seen as having on the growth and location of 'disruptive units'?

- What changes in youth custody rates occurred during the 1980s?

- What is the effect of including community homes within the framework of 'custodial measures' for children and young people who have committed offences?

- What does Mel Lloyd-Smith mean by a deviant career and how might a young person escape from one?

3.3 As well as providing us with information, the author puts forward a thesis about the consequences of intervention for what he calls 'deviants'. He echoes here some of the arguments about the labelling process from Unit 10. For Mel Lloyd-Smith, a 'deviant' is someone who has been categorized because of a breach of a school's or society's rules about correct behaviour. Increasing special provision for those who transgress school rules or society's laws directs attention and resources to the processes of identification and placement and may reduce an appreciation of causes and the effort required for the prevention of difficulties. In this way, not only are more young people identified as 'deviant' but schools and other institutions are reinforced in an approach to difficult behaviour which interprets it as caused solely by the failings of misbehaving individuals. This is a theme which will recur in other readings for this unit.

3.4 Does the growth of special provision correspond to a clear increase in disruptive behaviour or emotional upset in schools in the last decades? Although the claim that there is a rise in disorder in schools and elsewhere is a continuing refrain of some teachers and some of their unions, and some politicians and others, there is little evidence that this is the case. Geoffrey Pearson has documented the recurrence of the refrain, that disorder has reached unprecedented peaks, from the nineteenth century through to the 1980s (Pearson, 1983). However, Mel Lloyd-Smith does not offer much in the way of an alternative explanation apart from some sort of snowball effect of the labelling process. Once special units, for example, were seen as the solution to disorder in schools the reaction to continuing difficulties in schools was to provide more of them. The continuation of difficulties in schools might more logically have led to a challenge to the efficacy of special units as a solution.

3.5   The Pack Report, *Truancy and Indiscipline in Schools in Scotland* (Scottish Education Department, 1977) had recommended the use of disruptive units for dealing with 'challenging' students but some Scottish schools rejected this. The headteacher of one Glasgow school remarked that his teachers were 'only human' and would always be able to discover six more students they wished to be rid of. With his staff he set about establishing an alternative approach to difficult behaviour, involving student, parental and teacher collaboration through a system of 'school assessment panels' and the willingness to create individual timetables (Toppin, 1987).

3.6   Mel Lloyd-Smith makes a number of conjectures about the effects of the 1988 Act on the referral of troublesome students out of schools. In the years following the Act there has been a considerable growth in exclusions from schools and support services established to cope with difficulties in behaviour have been placed under considerable strain. I will have more to say about this later in the section.

3.7   Mel Lloyd-Smith reports a considerable drop in the use of youth custody throughout the 1980s. It appears to reflect satisfaction with non-custodial measures, despite the strong government law-and-order rhetoric of the same period.

3.8   You may have recalled the material on children in care in Unit 1/2 and be reminded that young people thought to have committed an offence can be sent to the same children's homes as children who have been abused by their parents or whose parents are unable to care for them. This may compound the assault on the identity of children taken into care and make it seem like a punishment for many of them.

3.9   The author sees a deviant career as life after labelling and argues that escape routes are rare. He may be a victim here of his subject matter. For in writing about such a wide range of provisions in relation to education and the courts he may be concentrating on only one group of young people and is too pessimistic about the extent to which students are able to change their status when they leave disruptive units, for example. And from his own figures the reconviction rates for young people convicted by the courts following non-custodial intervention is about 50 per cent, much lower than for custodial provision.

3.10   In Unit 1/2, I discussed the statementing procedures established by the 1981 Education Act. I indicated the variation in the proportions of the children and young people issued with statements in different LEAs. Within LEAs, too, different professionals interpret the statementing procedures differently and each statement represents a different compromise between the voices contributing to the outcome. The use of statementing procedures to decide on the education of and allocation of resources to students thought to have emotional problems and difficulties in behaviour which interfere with their learning is a particularly problematic area. It is made more so by the distinction that has been maintained over the years between disruptive students and those now referred to as having 'emotional and behavioural difficulties'. According to DES advice, a statement is not required for a student who is educated in a unit for 'disruptive pupils', either on or off the site of their school. This is so even though on any reading of the 1981 Act the education they receive would count as 'special educational provision'.

3.11   Frequently, recommendations for the transfer of students to units for disruptive students follow the exclusion of those students from particular lessons or from their school. This is not done because it is in the interests of the excluded student, although it might turn out to be, but because it is thought to be in the interests of the staff or other students.

3.12   It would be difficult to base a staementing procedure, supposedly related to the educational needs of the particular students with which it is concerned, on decisions taken about the needs and interests of others. Yet whether a student is seen as 'disruptive' or categorized as having 'emotional and behavioural difficulties' may be a matter of chance, depending on which particular professionals are involved and the availability of provision. It would be hard to maintain, then, that in all these cases the statementing procedures are carried out scrupulously in the interests of the students.

3.13   Now I do not think that education can or should raise the interests of students above the interests of teachers or that the interests of all students can be made compatible. However, I do think that the interests that are served should be made clear and where we are not running the system with the interests of the students uppermost then we have to take extra care that the system is not abused.

Activity 3   Perspectives on emotional and behavioural difficulties —

Derrick Armstrong and David Galloway have been studying statementing procedures for students referred to the schools psychological service because they were thought to have emotional and behavioural difficulties. They have reflected on some of their findings for us in Chapter 16 of Reader 2 'On being a client: conflicting perspectives on assessment'. The chapter extends the material on the statementing process in Unit 1/2 and on the relationship between parents and professionals in Unit 3/4. As you read the chapter consider whether, in contrast to the cases it describes, the categorization of a student as having emotional and behavioural difficulties could ever be a straightforward and unproblematic procedure.

3.14   The cases selected as typical of their findings by Derrick Armstrong and David Galloway highlight the processes that are occurring in this particular form of categorization. If it represented the interests of students or parents, we should expect to find that it was actively sought by them. Yet, as the three examples illustrate, in attaching the label there is a direct criticism of the child-rearing abilities of the parents.

3.15   Unlike the case of a child who is struggling with schoolwork, the concerns of the professionals and the solutions they offer to problems of emotional and behavioural difficulties hardly engage with the mentality of the parents. When reading about George, I was reminded of a play called *Hounds*, by the Graeae Theatre Company, which was based on blind people's experiences of guide-dog training centres. The dog's obedience and docility was compared to that of blind people who accept that they have to learn mobility in a remote centre isolated from the challenges of manoeuvring around their own environment. Faced with the problem of learning mobility, blind people themselves would never come up with the solution of such a remote training. It does not solve the problems of blind people, but those of charities for the blind and blindness professionals. Equally it is extremely unlikely that George's parents would discover that the solution to the family's difficulties was to send their son as a weekly boarder to a country house converted into a residential school for students assembled under the label of 'children with emotional and behavioural difficulties'. This is a solution to the educational psychologist's problem or to the difficulties of the school or LEA, but from the perspective of the parents or the child it may seem deranged.

3.16   Following the break-up of Tom's parents, Tom 'needs' his parents to sort out a new and stable way of relating to him. Would this adjustment be helped by coinciding with a school week in which lessons were disrupted on two half-days by his attendance at a 'disruptive unit', or more drastically with his removal from home and dispatch to a residential school?

3.17   The authors argue that the source of the power of parents is unlikely to be found in collaboration with the procedures themselves but in the extent to which they can find solutions by mobilizing alternative forms of support.

Responding to need? The Manor School, Wilburton, a day and residential school for students categorized as having emotional and behavioural difficulties. The school opened in 1953 at the tail end of government policy, after World War 2, to encourage local authorities to buy up country houses in order to expand boarding provision. It is situated ten miles from Cambridge and is the school which was attended by a pupil excluded from the Grove school, described in TV1, Under the Walnut Tree, *and Reader 2, p. 33.*

Categorization by gender, class and 'race'

3.18   The examples chosen by Derrick Armstrong and David Galloway to illustrate the categorization process are all concerned with boys. This reflects the overwhelming preponderance of boys in schools and units for students categorized as having 'emotional and behavioural difficulties'. According to a survey of such provision in England and Wales, boys outnumber girls by a factor of almost 6:1 (Cooper *et al.*, 1991). Some aspects of the relationship between gender and school difficulties are taken up in Section 5 of this unit. The way in which teachers respond differently to the challenging behaviour of girls and boys has been documented by Lyn Davies (1984).

3.19   Other studies have shown that the populations of schools and units for students categorized as deviant in behaviour are overwhelmingly working class (Ford, Mongon and Whelan, 1982; Tomlinson, 1982). This finding leads me to question whether the provision for students categorized as disruptive *or* as having emotional and behavioural difficulties could survive if a majority of the students were middle class. This has particular force given the poor level of resources and narrowed curricula found in such schools and units (DES, 1989b; SOED, 1990). Is it possible in our society, then, for the majority of students categorized as difficult in their behaviour to be middle class?

3.20   In their research, Paul Cooper, Graham Upton, and Colin Smith paid particular attention to the ethnic distribution of categorized students. A comparison of their representation as a percentage of the total population of young people and of the percentage of students in schools and units for 'emotional and behavioural difficulties' is shown in Table 1.

Table 1   Representation of young people (up to age 19 years) by ethnic origin (percentages).

Ethnic origin	Total population	Schools and units for emotional and behavioural difficulties
Afro-Caribbean	2.4	4.8
Indian	6.7	0.5
Pakistani	2.9	1.4
Bangladeshi	0.1	0.03
White European	86.0	92.0
Other	1.7	1.3

3.21   Table 1 indicates a considerable over-representation of students of Afro-Caribbean origin and an under-representation of Asian origin students, particularly those with an Indian background. As the authors of the study point out, students of Afro-Caribbean origin are also over-represented in the working-class population. Is there a multiplier effect whereby stereotypic views of working-class and Afro-Caribbean culture combine so that teachers see these students as in opposition to schools' values? I will take up these issues further in examining figures for exclusions from school.

The perspective of the special school

3.22   The examination of the vagaries and biases of categorization procedures can seem irrelevant from the perspective of those who work within segregated special provision. Those of you who work within special schools may teach students who arrive at your schools because they have been rejected by or inappropriately supported within their mainstream schools and families. The correction of the failings of the mainstream may be psychologically and physically remote, particularly for those who work in residential settings. Ted Cole (1986) has written a supportive book about 'residential special education', written from his perspective in the independent sector. Yet to those planning provision within a particular local authority, aware of the great practical difficulties of providing a broad stimulating education in small schools for groups of 'challenging' and rejected students (DES, 1989b), often remote from their homes, alternative solutions to mainstream failure may seem more attractive. These alternatives and the problems they encounter will be explored further in Section 6 of this unit.

3.23   In the early 1990s there is strong evidence that the number of students excluded from school because of difficulties with their behaviour is rising steeply. Some argue that this is caused by increasing turmoil in students while others attribute it to the increasing pressures on schools associated with the 1988 Education Act, particularly local management of schools (LMS) and the publishing of pupils' exam and test results. A further group see the cause as a delay, in some schools, in finding a viable alternative to corporal punishment as a last resort for controlling student behaviour.

3.24   Exclusions are regulated in England and Wales by the 1986 Education Act, sections 23–7, which permits a headteacher to exclude a student for a fixed term, indefinitely or permanently. A child may be excluded for five days or less in one term without informing the school governors or the LEA, although parents must be told 'without delay'. Above this period, or if the exclusion will affect the student taking a public examination, the head must inform the governors and the LEA of the decision and the parents (or the pupil if he or she is over eighteen) of their right of appeal against it. A pupil under eighteen can still appeal themselves though their parents have the right to be involved. The governors and LEA must be told, too, if the exclusion is changed from a fixed or indefinite period to a permanent exclusion.

3.25   Both school governors and LEAs have powers to confirm the exclusion or reinstate students at the excluding school. If the LEA and governors suggest different dates for reinstatement, the headteacher must act on the earlier date. LEAs must also enable parents to appeal against a decision not to reinstate the student and governors can appeal against an LEA decision to send the student back to school. This last possibility was added to the Act in response to the action of teachers at Poundswick School in Manchester, many of whom stayed on strike for a school year in protest at the decision of Manchester Council to reinstate five students accused of daubing the walls with racist, sexist and sexually explicit graffiti directed against members of the school staff (see Booth, 1987).

3.26   Exclusions only affect a small proportion of the school population (around 2 per cent), though until 1992 there had been no national survey of exclusion rates. While this unit was being prepared, the DES was gathering information from all LEAs in England but only on permanent exclusions (the survey may be published in 1993; the Welsh Office is conducting its own survey). The rising problem has been exposed through TV and radio programmes, by the Association of Educational Psychologists and by researchers. The *You and Yours* Radio 4 programme of 29 January 1992 conducted an informal survey of a dozen LEAs. All those that recorded details had found an increase, with particularly high rises in Newcastle, Glamorgan and Birmingham. Stephen Byers, chair of the Education Committee of the Association of Metropolitan Authorities, reported on his committee's findings in the same programme:

It's a national problem. It's happening throughout the country. In Newcastle there's been something like a 50 per cent increase from one year to the next ... What's particularly worrying is the number of exclusions in the primary sector. You wouldn't have thought that those pupils aged 5–11 would be subject to exclusions. To go back to Newcastle again, there's been 30 per cent increase in primary school exclusions from one year to the next. The same in Leeds; a big increase in primary school exclusions. It's a trend that should give all of us concern.

(*You and Yours*, 29 January 1992)

3.27   A *Public Eye* programme broadcast on 3 May 1991 also conducted a survey, this time of sixty LEAs, with the great majority reporting an increase in permanent exclusions. A number of people supported the argument that the rise in exclusions was due to competitive pressures brought in by the 1988 Education Act. Paul White, although himself a Conservative, and chair of the Council of Local Education Authorities argued that the encouragement to schools to opt out would produce a two-tier education system with opted-out schools rejecting difficult students. One headteacher argued that 'the special needs youngster is likely to demand more than their share of resources and is likely to threaten the image of the school'. She argued that she might take decisions on 'marketing terms', when deciding which children to accept at her school.

3.28   Contrary to the beliefs of many, Michael Fallon, then schools minister, argued that the 1988 Act was not meant to exert selective pressures and that schools were expected 'to meet the needs of the whole community':

> What we haven't altered is the legal responsibility of LEAs to assess the needs of children and to ensure that appropriate provision is made to meet those needs. There is nothing in the local management of schools or in the moves to grant maintained status (opting out) that is going to alter that legal obligation. Local education authorities will retain that obligation and it's up to them to fulfil it.

(Michael Fallon, *Public Eye*, 3 May 1991)

However, Michael Fallon seemed to be unaware of the problems of many LEAs who find they have decreasing power to enforce the fulfilment of the legal responsibilities they retain. I will discuss this further in Section 6 in considering the plight of behaviour support services. As you will see, the problem of exclusions is a major theme of this unit. It surfaces, as well, in relation to truancy in the next section and in regard to fears some teachers had about the abolition of corporal punishment which are mentioned in Section 5.

3.29   In her research into the effects of the 1988 Education Act on students seen to have emotional and behavioural difficulties, Margaret Stirling encountered a further problem about exclusions. Despite the apparently clear guidelines of the 1986 Education Act, many excluded students were not notified to the LEA. This was particularly apparent for the vulnerable children in children's homes:

> Of 60 young people in 7 children's homes in one of the authorities studied, 32 were excluded from school. Of these 32, only 2 could be readily identified by my respondents as officially excluded and so recorded as the responsibility of the LEA. This LEA acknowledges that 300 pupils in its area are officially excluded. *If the ratio of officially known to unknown suspensions I found in the sample quoted above were to be representative of the whole authority, then we are talking not of 300 children but of thousands. Throughout my research professionals consulted have consistently reported that relatively few of the out of school children they work with were recorded as permanently excluded.*
>
> (Stirling, 1992, p. 9)

Margaret Stirling does not seem to realize that schools are meant to notify an LEA about exclusions totalling more than five days in any one term. However, she highlights the need to compare the official figures produced by an LEA with the reality of exclusions in particular schools. How might one set about making such a check?

3.30   Like others, she found that the rise in exclusions was being fuelled by beliefs about the competitive pressures of the 1988 Act:

> Mainstream heads interviewed were all concerned that the publication of test results, required by the National Curriculum [*sic*], should give a favourable impression of their school. One principal educational psychologist reflected the opinion of many interviewed: 'The recognized success of schools, their public profiles, is making the difference. Allied to the numbers of pupils coming into schools is the money coming in. So the more "successful" a school is seen to be the more kids it will attract and therefore the more money it will attract. Kids who screw up the formula are not going to be encouraged.'
>
> (Stirling, 1992, p. 8)

Financial considerations were leading heads to exclude students. They were not prepared to wait for the possible financial benefits that might be provided by the statementing process.

Exclusion and black students

3.31   The exclusion figures that have been released by LEAs are unbalanced in a number of ways. There is an overwhelming preponderance of boys and there is often an over-representation of black students of Afro-Caribbean origin (Birmingham City Council, 1991; Nottinghamshire County Council, 1991; London Borough of Lewisham, 1991). The report from Birmingham City Council is particularly interesting and worrying because in 1983 the Commission on Racial Equality published an investigation into 'referral and suspension' in Birmingham schools prompted by concerns about the high numbers of black students excluded in the late 1970s (CRE, 1983). The investigation found that up to 1979 there was a considerable over-representation of

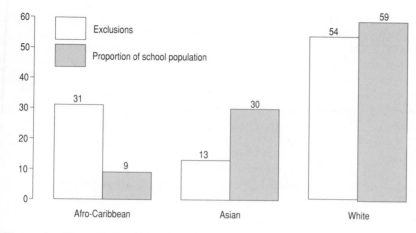

Figure 1   Permanent exclusions by ethnic group compared with proportion of school population (percentages) (source: data from Birmingham City Council, 1991, para. 3.5).

students 'of West-Indian origin'. But by the time of the report, the rate of 'black suspension' was 'close to the proportion of black pupils in the Birmingham school population'. It was felt that a variety of education and community services had made successful interventions. However, a report of the Chief Education Officer to the Education (Special Needs and Welfare Sub-) Committee of the Council revealed that the 1991 figures for permanent exclusions had returned to their 1979 biases (Birmingham City Council, 1991). Figure 1 gives the percentage of the permanent exclusions for different groupings compared with their proportion of the total school population.

3.32   These figures are comparable to those obtained in Nottinghamshire and Lewisham and elsewhere. Students from Asian backgrounds are far less likely to be excluded, while students from Afro-Caribbean backgrounds are far more likely to be excluded, than would be indicated by their representation in the population as a whole. Why is this so? That the relationship between teachers and students of Afro-Caribbean origin is sometimes marked by conflict is clear from the figures. Is it that such students, for reasons which may include rebellion against a devalued status, are actually more disruptive?

3.33   David Gillborn carried out a careful study in one school, observing many lessons and talking to students and teachers. It was an area with a high incidence of black students. He found that 'Afro-Caribbean students were frequently criticized for behaviour which other students shared in but for which white and Asian students were not criticized' (Gillborn, 1992, p. 6). He described an incident involving Paul Dixon and his close friend Arif Aslam:

> On one occasion both Paul Dixon (Afro-Caribbean) and Arif Aslam (Asian) arrived seven minutes late for a mixed-ability lesson which I observed. They apologized for the delay but explained that they had been with the head of guidance. Almost half an hour into the lesson

most of the group were working steadily and, like the majority of their peers, Paul and Arif were holding a conversation while they worked. The teacher looked up from the pupil he was dealing with and shouted across the room: 'Paul. Look, you come in late, now you have the audacity to waste not only your time but his [Arif's] as well.' The fact that both Paul and Arif had arrived late, and that the conversation was a two-way affair was not reflected in the teacher's statement which explicitly criticized the Afro-Caribbean pupil while implying that his Asian friend was a blameless victim.

(Gillborn, 1992, pp. 30–31)

3.34   Other students confirmed David Gillborn's observation that Afro-Caribbean students were frequently and unfairly criticized. In response to the sentence completion task '......... is picked on by some teachers', half of the pupils nominated 'were of Afro-Caribbean origin'. (Gillborn, 1990, p. 31). In an interview, one student, a white girl, referred specifically to Paul Dixon:

> DG Do you think that any groups of pupils are treated differently in the school?
>
> VICKY Yeah, I mean Paul Dixon (...) I could cause trouble as well as him, if something went wrong while the teacher wasn't there, they'd probably try and blame him, when it could've been *me*.
>
> (...) Paul and people like that, you know, if they really do settle down to their work then the teacher'd say, 'Oh, what's wrong with you, *you're working!*' And taking it out on them then *'cause they are working*. And I suppose he thinks 'Why bother ... they're always getting at me'. I feel sorry for him in a way.
>
> (Gillborn, 1990, p. 60)

3.35   David Gillborn argued that teachers adopted 'the myth of an Afro-Caribbean challenge – the teachers' widespread belief that, both as individuals and as a group, Afro-Caribbean pupils were especially prone to threatening teachers' authority' (Gillborn, 1990, p. 57). The example of one student who, eventually, was permanently excluded from the school, was carefully documented. In the third year Wayne's year head described the *feeling* staff had about him:

> I have him for [one lesson], for instance, and I don't hear a word out of him, he just gets on with the work. But there are other areas of the school where, if you give him half an inch, he'll take a mile (...) You name it, he's done it.
>
> (Gillborn, 1990, p. 57)

3.36   When Wayne was finally excluded it was for a series of incidents, none of which was 'so serious that it would normally have brought about expulsion'. After Wayne had left school, his form teacher summarized the challenge to authority that he had represented:

> Wayne Johnson was just somebody who we tried and tried and tried with ... School wasn't the place for him with his *inner drive*, as

I saw it, to always appear to be number one, and unbowed by any authority ... Our institution just couldn't brook that kind of continual challenge ...

(Gillborn, 1990, p. 59)

3.37   David Gillborn, noticed that teachers were affronted by certain cultural behaviours of the Afro-Caribbean students, for example, a habit of looking down when reprimanded. They also saw styles of walking as expressing hostility. Maud Blair made similar observations in her study in schools with relatively few black students. She explained how one girl told her of an incident that occurred as she and her brother were walking into school in what was for them a natural and relaxed way:

A teacher who had a very poor relationship with most of the Black pupils, and certainly with this one, grabbed her brother by his shirt front, raised him above the ground, held him against the wall, and said, 'I am going to rid you of this need to show off if it's the last thing I do. Now go back and don't come in until you've learned to walk properly'. The boy, a fourth year (or Year 10), humiliated in front of the other pupils and considering this to be unjust anyway, was not going to oblige the teacher *and* lose face by meekly obeying these orders, so he simply walked out of the school, thereby breaking an important rule. The whole situation escalated to the point where he was eventually given a temporary suspension.

(Blair, 1991, p. 5)

3.38   Such teachers may not make the overtly racist remarks described in some studies (see Schostak, 1983; Wright, 1987). Yet their unwillingness to question their ethnocentric assumptions about displays of power and deference makes them as effectively racist. Until such attitudes and other devaluations of Afro-Caribbean students are recognized and countered they will continue to swell the exclusion figures and at a time of rapidly rising exclusion rates such students are particularly vulnerable. The pressures from the Education Reform Act seem to be making schools less ready to tolerate diversity of attainment and behaviour. Overzealousness about conformity is inevitably ethnocentric and discriminatory. The rise in exclusions and the over-representation of black students may be reminders that such pushes to uniformity should be resisted.

4   OPTING OUT: TRUANTING FROM SCHOOL

4.1   Some students escape from the day-to-day control of the school and classroom by absenting themselves from school. In doing so they may set in train another set of control procedures associated with what one writer has called 'the truancy industry' (Wardhaugh, 1990). 'The truancy industry' is composed of the medical, educational, social work and legal professionals who are involved in assessing, chasing, cajoling or 'caring' for young people who absent themselves from school.

4.2   Most people who write about truancy see it as 'bad behaviour'. Yet there are others, not all of whom are students or their parents, who do not see schools as the best place to acquire an education. Shaw wrote of schools as prisons, a view echoed later when I come to consider student accounts of truancy:

> There is nothing on earth intended for innocent people so horrible as a school. To begin with, it is a prison. But it is in some respects more cruel than a prison. In a prison, for instance, you are not forced to read books written by the warders and governor. In prison they may torture your body; but they do not torture your brains.
>
> (Shaw, 1921, pp. 30–31)

4.3   Eric Blyth and Judith Milner, lecturers in social work, see truants as arising from the ranks of 'the large minority of children for whom education is at best an irrelevance and at worst a totally humiliating experience' (Blyth and Milner, 1987). For these authors, then, truanting may be a rational response to impoverished social and educational conditions found in schools. As we shall see, these authors are following in a tradition of giving a simple generalization as the reason for truancy. Nevertheless, it does make sense to ask whether we need to explain why some students absent themselves from school or why so few do so.

4.4   I will start this section by discussing the way truancy is and should be defined. I will ask whether truancy could occur without the requirement for compulsory education. I will consider the number of students who are absent from school and how this has changed over the years and the proportion of these students who are absent 'without official justification'. I will then examine the variety of explanations that are offered for truancy both by teachers and education writers and by students themselves. I will assess the responses that have been made to truancy in the recommendations of the Elton enquiry on discipline in schools (DES, 1989a) and by government and examine the changing role of the education welfare service.

WHAT IS TRUANCY?

4.5   Truancy has to be understood in the context of compulsory education. The possibility of illegal absence arose with the 1876 Education Act which added compulsion up to the age of twelve to the universal provision of primary education brought in by the Education Act of 1870. Subsequently the Education Acts of 1918 and 1944 made school attendance compulsory for all young people up to the age of sixteen, though the provision within the 1944 Act for schooling to last for five years of secondary schooling was only finally implemented with an 'Order in Council' by the Conservative administration of 1972 (Simon, 1991).

26

4.6   Attendance at school is still regulated in England and Wales by the 1944 Education Act which makes it clear that it is education rather than attendance at school that is compulsory. (Broadly similar requirements are set out for Scotland in the Education (Scotland) Acts of 1962 and 1980.)

> It shall be the duty of the parent of every child of compulsory school age to cause him [sic] to receive efficient full-time education suitable to his age, ability and aptitude either by regular attendance at school or otherwise.
>
> (Education Act 1944, Section 36)

4.7   If it is education rather than schooling that is compulsory, why do the efforts to curb truancy concentrate on ensuring that students attend school rather than on ensuring an appropriate education when they get there? The 1944 Act also places a duty on local education authorities to ensure that parents are fulfilling their obligations:

> If it appears ... that the parent of any child of compulsory school age is failing to perform the duty imposed on him [sic], it shall be the duty of the authority to serve upon the parent a notice requiring him ... to satisfy the authority that the child is receiving efficient full-time education suitable to his age, ability, and aptitude ... then, if in the opinion of the authority it is expedient that he should attend school, the authority shall serve upon the parent an order ... requiring him to cause the child to become a registered pupil at a school named in the order.
>
> (Education Act 1944, Section 37)

Under the Pupils' Registration Regulations of 1956 all schools must take a register at the beginning of morning and afternoon sessions and these have been amended by the Education (Pupils' Attendance Records) Regulations 1991 to require teachers to indicate whether a particular absence is 'authorized' (carries a legitimate excuse) or 'unauthorized' (DES, 1991).

4.8   Other things being equal, the authority is required to accept a parent's choice of school. Parents who fail to ensure that their children are in full-time education can be fined by the magistrates court or, in theory, may be imprisoned after a third conviction. In practice the law has assumed that the father should be prosecuted unless the mother has sole custody (Poole, 1987).

4.9   Before the 1990s an LEA could also apply to the juvenile court under Section 1(2) of the 1969 Children and Young Person's Act for a young person to be taken into care because of their poor attendance, although the alternative of a social work supervision order was the more common outcome. The 1989 Children Act has curtailed LEAs' power to institute care proceedings and has introduced Education Supervision Orders. The education welfare officer, who is usually expected to undertake the supervision, is required to 'advise, assist and befriend *and give directions to* ...' (my emphasis) a child and his or her parents in order to 'secure that' the child 'is properly educated' (Children Act 1989,

Schedule 3, Part III). The order remains in force for a year but can be extended by the court for up to three years. It is still possible for absence from school to be considered as a factor in care proceedings brought by a social services department if it is considered that a young person is out of parental control or at risk of physical or psychological harm.

4.10 Parents can make three main defences against prosecution for the non-attendance of their child apart from the granting of 'leave' by the school:

(a) at any time when he was prevented from attending by reason of sickness or any unavoidable cause;

(b) on any day exclusively set apart for religious observance by the religious body to which his parents belong;

(c) if the parent proves that the school at which the child is a registered pupil is not within walking distance of the child's home, and that no suitable arrangements have been made by the local education authority ...

(Education Act 1944, Section 39)

However, when cases reach the court, parents usually plead guilty. A series of court cases have helped to pin down the legal definition of full-time attendance at school. Parents have been fined for sanctioning a few days' illicit absence and lateness of a student for school can also lead to parental prosecution (Grimshaw and Pratt, 1987). But the term 'truancy' itself is not defined legally and different people use it in different ways.

4.11 In any further reading you do, you should be aware of the lack of consensus on definitions. Different definitions lead to different estimates of incidence as well as different explanations of truancy. Some definitions obtain 'official' backing because of their use in government documents. The Elton Report (DES, 1989a), for example, distinguishes parentally 'condoned absence', which accounts for the majority of illicit absence (Reid, 1987), from 'truancy' and draws attention to 'internal truancy' whereby pupils stay around the school but miss some of their lessons. Is it sensible to complicate the notion of truancy by limiting it to absence which is regarded as illegitimate by the school authorities and which is not condoned by parents? Wouldn't it be simpler to regard as truancy all absence for which there is no adequate medical, religious or other excuse which exempts a parent from prosecution?

4.12 There is a further complicating factor in not regarding parentally condoned absence as a form of truancy since parents are not the only people who condone absence. As the Elton Report recognized, some teachers are relieved when students that they find particularly challenging are not present in their classes: 'It has been suggested to us that the non-attendance of certain pupils may actually help to improve general behaviour in some schools' (DES, 1989a, p. 166). Schools may contribute actively to the absence of students, too, when students whose attendance is not welcomed are punished on their return to school. I had thought that stories of young people being excluded from school for truancy were apocryphal until I checked with the chief education welfare officer in my area who assured me that this had happened in several local education authorities. I also discovered that 'absconding from school/poor attendance' was a reason (albeit the least common reason) for excluding students, uncovered by the NUT survey on exclusions (NUT, 1992).

4.13   If we accept truancy as defined exclusively by illicit absence then we can further subdivide it into a number of categories in terms of the pattern of absence, the degree to which it is supported by parents or by the characteristics of the children and young people concerned. I would wish, for example, to separate persistent or prolonged absence from occasional absence, though an arbitrary cut-off would be required in defining them. The categorization of students into types of truants is bound up inextricably with the reasons given for truancy and I will deal with it below after looking at the numbers involved.

4.14   I have suggested that we define truancy in relation to compulsory schooling, but would we cease to be interested in it if schooling were voluntary? It would be decriminalized and parents would not be fined because of it. But since most parents want their children to attend school, non-attendance would continue to be a problem for them. If the students in the catchment area of a particular school voted with their feet, against the value of the education offered, then it would be in the interest of staff to attempt to recapture their enthusiasm. I don't know what decriminalization of school attendance would do for school attendance figures. I think most children want to go to school and I do not think they go only because they have to legally. I think there is a cultural imperative to do so. I do know that schools with sixth forms differ markedly in their staying on rates after the compulsory school years. But without the legal requirement for school attendance, how would we define truancy? Would we have to reinvent some form of compulsion for parents to fulfil their children's right to education?

HOW MANY CHILDREN AND YOUNG PEOPLE TRUANT?

4.15   As things are, nationally, about 10 per cent of school students are absent from school on any one day. The figures vary regionally, from school to school and with the age of students. Wales, for example, has had higher rates, and the incidence is greater in inner cities than suburbs and rural areas. Of the number absent, only a minority are absent without a legitimate excuse and only a small minority of these are persistently absent. However, as you may recall from Unit 1/2, travellers are a special case in this respect. About 50 per cent of primary age travellers attend school and this drops to between 10 and 20 per cent at secondary age.

4.16   The figure of about 90 per cent attendance has been surprisingly stable over the years. David Galloway looked through the attendance records for the City of Sheffield and found that the attendance levels in the mid-1970s differed little from those in the early part of the century (Galloway, 1985). However, compulsory education now encompasses a much older age group and it is remarkable that this has been accomplished without a dramatic increase in truancy.

4.17   Attendance varies between schools and decreases with age. As discussed in the Elton Report, an ILEA survey in 1987 revealed variation in secondary school attendance rates between 94.3 per cent and 63.6 per cent. The average rate for 11-year-olds was 90.3 per cent while for 15-year-olds it was 70 per cent. The report also quoted an HMI survey which stressed that the lower rates were not confined to schools serving disadvantaged areas (DES, 1989a). If figures vary so markedly with age and between schools in similar areas for children of the same age then it can be argued that the difference between the best and the worst attendance records in these cases are attributable to unjustified absence. Thus the ILEA figures could mean that at least 20 per cent of 15-year-olds are unjustifiably absent. If we look instead at the numbers of students who admit deliberately avoiding some lessons the numbers are far higher. In one survey 52 per cent of students in their final year of compulsory schooling admitted playing truant for the odd lesson here or there (Gray and Clough, 1984).

4.18   David Galloway (1985) reported on a number of surveys of persistent absentees in the city of Sheffield. He adopted a particularly severe criterion for persistent absence, defining it as less than 50 per cent of possible attendance in any one term. On this criterion, 0.4 per cent of primary age pupils were persistently absent but in some schools the rate had risen to 10 per cent by the final year of compulsory schooling. At primary level roughly similar numbers of girls and boys were absent. At secondary level, 'there was a slight, but consistent, tendency for more girls than boys to be recorded as persistent unauthorized absentees' (Galloway, 1985, p. 17). However, very few of these girls were absent without parental consent.

WHO ARE THE TRUANTS?

4.19   As I have suggested, divisions according to the characteristics of students always imply explanations for truancy. Over the years, certain stereotypes of students who truant have emerged in writings which colour our view of truancy. This can lead to an odd disjunction between our own experience and the view of truancy in books and articles. Fiona Paterson has conducted a historical and sociological study of truancy in her book, *Out of Place* (Paterson, 1989). The title reflects her definition of truancy as not being where you're supposed to be. For her, truancy is an ordinary breach of rules by students often acting rationally and sensibly. Her study reflects a puzzle that she uncovers when she compares the way truancy is defined in the literature with her own memories of school:

> I went to a local secondary school which was attended by children who were considered to be the academic successes of the school system. I was aware that many, though by no means all, of my peers truanted. In other ways, those who truanted were no different from those who did not – some did well in exams, others did not; some were middle class, others were working class; most conformed, more or less, when they were in school, some did not conform. Truanting was an activity in which people engaged to varying degrees (at times skipping individual classes, at times taking half or full days off) and at different times of the year (sometimes taking illicit time off to prepare for an exam, to enjoy the sunshine on a summer day or simply to do something more interesting than go to school).

> Yet much later, when I came across the Pack Report on Truancy and Indiscipline in Schools [SED, 1977], I did not recognize the picture of children described there. Turning from this to the literature on truancy, I still failed to find the image which I remembered from my school days. As a sociologist I was aware that the images of truancy about which I was reading, with their standard fare of education failure, 'deprived' backgrounds and problem families, reflected discussions of other types of social problem. This led me to consider the gap between my 'knowledge' based on my school experience and the orthodox 'knowledge' which I could receive from books and articles about truancy and which were clearly based in a different kind of experience to my own.

> (Paterson, 1989, p. vii)

4.20   However, a concern about selective truancy, which has existed since the origin of schools, has made periodic reappearances as if it was a new phenomenon, although not everyone sees it in the same positive light as Fiona Paterson. I have noticed references to new waves of selective truancy in the media in the early 1990s. The Ralphs Report on the education welfare services noted it twenty years earlier: 'the quite different pattern of habitual absence from school for one or two days a week by large numbers of children suggests an indifference to the value of education which has the gravest of implications' (Local Government Training Board, 1973, para. 34). In practice, only some students who truant may find themselves labelled or regarded as 'truants'. Who is regarded as a 'truant' depends on cultural attitudes as well as more idiosyncratic views within particular schools and local education authorities. Some authorities have no educational welfare service whose job it is to intervene in cases of truancy and these different patterns of surveillance affect the school and later careers of school absentees.

4.21   In her analysis of the literature on truancy, Fiona Paterson claims to detect three main themes concerned with 'the fearful truant or child with school phobia, the endangered truant and the disaffected truant'. The first of these two categories locate the 'problem' within the child and his or her family, whilst the third permits the possibility that truancy might arise because of deficiencies in schools and the way they reflect cultural values placed on students.

4.22   I can see the necessity for a separate category of 'emotional avoidance of school or school phobia'. School phobia provides a medically certifiable justification for absence from school and exempts parents from prosecution (see Blagg, 1987). Having witnessed the terror of some students as they approach the school gates or set out on a journey to school, I would not wish to dispute the reality of the pain felt by some young people and would see this emotional reaction as arising for a variety of reasons at school and at home.

4.23   However, the distinction between fearful (i.e. students with school phobia) and non-fearful truants is not so easy to maintain in practice and the way the problems of some students are defined can give credence to the view that 'the school phobic is simply a middle-class truant' (Wardhaugh, 1990, p. 755). In Felicity Armstrong's interviews with teachers about truancy, one teacher described the very different ways in which two primary school students were regarded in the same school, on the advice of the same educational psychologist:

> One boy was treated with great sensitivity by the teachers at the school and by the educational psychologist. It was decided that he was suffering from 'school phobia' and was allowed to arrive after the other children and attend lessons if he felt able to. If he preferred he could read or work in the school library. He was referred to a psychiatric unit (by an educational psychologist) where he and his family received counselling.

> At the same period another boy of similar age (11) was experiencing difficulties in attendance. He would arrive at the back entrance of the school with his mother; he was crying and distressed. A teacher would sometimes come and help the mother 'escort' the boy into the classroom under the watchful eyes of the rest of the class. He was talked to in a manner which was kind and firm as he was physically dragged towards his desk. Sometimes he would break free and run off. The same educational psychologist saw this boy. He did not refer him for any special help. He explained the legal position to the mother who became increasingly terrified she would be taken to court and her son would be 'put in a home' or she would be fined. This boy was seen as a 'truant' and spoilt and manipulative.

> The parents of the first boy were college lecturers. The mother of the second boy was single and worked part-time in a shop. Two years later both boys are still having difficulty in attending school. In the first case the problem is seen as a psychiatric one within the child and his family. In the second case the problem is seen as a social/behavioural one within the child and possibly extending to

the mother. Both boys say they 'hate' school and yet no-one has examined factors within school which might be causing them to feel this.

(Teacher talking to Felicity Armstrong, 1992, personal communication)

4.24   Julia Wardhaugh studied the educational welfare service in a local authority she calls Norwest. From the accounts of individual welfare officers she found she could fit a group of students into Fiona Paterson's endangered category. The accounts revealed a set of stereotyped attitudes and judgements. Sometimes, sexual abuse was not taken seriously and the victim was seen as contributing to it. Boys were seen as more likely to engage in criminal activity and girls were seen as at risk of sexual exploitation from an abusing family or others:

> Ian is criminal and has got criminal friends. He just does not want to go to school. His father is an alcoholic and the mother wears the trousers. She won't have him taken into care. He is going to court and will end up in a detention centre probably.
> (pp. 747–8)

> Melanie was sexually abused by her father, though I'm not sure how far it went. He's of very low intelligence so I don't think he really knew what he was doing. Now, when he tries to make her attend school she threatens she will get the social services on to him, so you see really he is scared to do anything about her truanting.
> (p. 746)

> I asked Mrs Jones why she had nine kids and she just said 'he likes his drink and I like sex, I just get caught every time'. What can you expect of the daughters when the mother talks like that? There's a case of a 13 year old girl, Stephanie, her mother knows she's having sex with her boyfriend. She's obviously in moral danger and should be taken into care for her own protection.
> (p. 749–50)

> (Wardhaugh, 1990)

4.25   The preoccupation of male education welfare officers with the sexuality of women and girls was noted by Julia Wardhaugh: 'No references were made during many of the cases discussed by the Norwest EWS to the moral welfare of males, either fathers or sons. Evidently it was seen as 'normal' that they should be sexually active' (p. 750). The impact of stereotypic attitudes towards the gender and social class of students is elaborated further by Julia Wardhaugh and others in Carlen, Gleason and Wardhaugh (1992). While the above accounts convey a picture of the 'delinquent' or 'morally endangered truant', a different picture emerges from a more general investigation of truancy. There is a dispute about whether truants are particularly likely to indulge in petty crime. Some writers claim to have found a clear association (e.g. Berg *et al.*, 1985), while others maintain that the evidence does not support a connection (Paterson, 1988; Wardhaugh, 1990). They would all agree that the great majority of school absentees do not engage in crime and therefore do not truant in order to do so.

4.26 It might be obvious to answer the question, 'Why did you truant?', with, 'Because I didn't want to go to school.' However, this answer has received very little attention in writings on truancy over the years. Would we be more inclined to consider it if schooling were voluntary? And what of the answer to the question, 'Why *didn't* you truant?'

4.27 The most common explanation for truancy has been in terms of the inadequacies of parents and, as we have seen, the law focuses on parental responsibility. Writing in 1891, Mary Tabor observed:

> The bulk of persistent irregularity, with all its worry to the teacher, injury to the child and waste of the public money, is chargeable to neglect. In some of the lower grade schools the list of absentees counts up regularly to 30 per cent or even more of the numbers on the roll; and the worst cases, with but few exceptions, are those with drunken and idle parents. It is not the children who are at fault, the teachers and attendance officers tell us. In 19 cases out of 20 it is the parents; father, mother, or both; drink-sodden, lazy or neglectful people, who will not bear the trouble to rise, give the children a meal, and send them off, willing or unwilling, until past the hour when the school doors are closed.
>
> (Tabor, 1891, p. 512)

4.28 This view of the truant as a child of feckless parents has found supporters, consistently, over the years. Writing nearly eighty years later, Tyerman described families and attributed responsibility for truancy in similar terms:

> In more than three-quarters of the cases the parents set poor examples and had low standards. They neglected their children, were ineffective in their supervision, and took little interest in their welfare. The view of many writers that the truant is born into an inferior environment seemed to be confirmed.
>
> (Tyerman, 1968, p. 58)

4.29 A number of researchers have found that persistent long-term truancy is strongly associated with family poverty. And provided we define truancy in this stringent way an association with disadvantaged circumstances is revealed, consistently. But there is a considerable leap from finding an association between disadvantaged circumstances and persistent absenteeism to reaching a conclusion that it is parental inadequacy which causes truancy. It is a complex process to disentangle the combinations of economic and family circumstances which occur in the homes of some persistent absentees and to decide whether responsibility for the absences should be assigned to them. Persistent absence may reflect the priorities of children and their parents as a rational response to their circumstances and the possibilities of school attendance for changing them. This was argued by David Galloway in interpreting the results of his research:

> ... the problem of school attendance was often treated in the same way as a demand for payment of an electricity bill or a hire purchase demand – something to be deferred as long as possible. For a majority of families, living in multiply disadvantaged, acutely stressful circumstances, school attendance was low on the list of priorities. For parents the higher priorities were more basic: housing, heating, food, their own health and the health of their children. Many parents simply lacked the energy to pack a reluctant child off to school. The children, too, regarded school attendance as a low priority when faced with the more immediate problem of a chronically depressed parent, younger brothers and sisters who needed looking after, food that needed to be bought.
>
> (Galloway, 1985, p. 75)

4.30 And if it is the inadequacies of parents and backgrounds that are to blame for truancy, why do these fail to manifest themselves at primary school and become increasingly significant as students progress through their secondary schools? Some older students may be absent in order to contribute to the family economy by earning money or looking after younger children. But David Galloway sees another possible explanation behind this fact:

> It is not in dispute that fifteen- and sixteen-year-olds are more frequently absent than younger age groups. The fact that fifteen- and sixteen-year-olds from economically disadvantaged families are more likely than any other group to be absent does not alter this point. Logically, the increasing absenteeism throughout the secondary school years could be caused by pressures in society and/or their families which affect adolescents more than children ... Yet it would be absurd and irresponsible not also to investigate the possibility that the climate and curriculum of many secondary schools plays a central part in the sharp increase in absence rates from these schools compared with primary schools.
>
> (Galloway, 1985, p. 53)

4.31 As I have mentioned, it has also been repeatedly noted that schools in similar catchment areas differ in their truancy rates. One possible, and unsurprising, conclusion would be that students find some schools more attractive to attend than others. That difficulties with lessons and teachers prompt some students to be absent from schools is a repeated refrain of students themselves, though some see such reasoning as merely an excuse: 'It is unwise to accept truants' excuses at their face value. The limits of self-deception are wide and it is easier to blame other people than oneself ... Parents and children look for a scapegoat and the teacher is often chosen' (Tyerman, 1968, p. 73).

4.32 If the 'limits of self-deception are wide' perhaps we need to look carefully at our own motives when we blame the problem of truancy solely on young people and their families. One of the deceptions to which authors succumb is that a single factor or a few simple ones will provide an explanation of truancy. If it's not the home, it must be the school:

> Teachers ... tend to be unaware of their own part and that of their school in the process. They are inclined to blame everybody, parents, pupils, social services departments and society – in fact, everybody but themselves – when their pupils miss school. This is not only wrong, it is ignorant.
>
> (Reid, 1987, p. 208)

Students' views

> I do not like fighting and I like listening to records. I liked school a little bit. When I dodged school I did not do what the rest of them do I went fishing as it is my best past time and I also done some sports.
>
> (Steelworker in Gow and McPherson, 1980, p. 44)

4.33   We might expect that 'bad schools and teachers' would be a common explanation for truancy from students, though we might need to think carefully about the kind of truancy we were looking at before we could expect a particular explanation to be frequent. However, when Roger Grimshaw and John Pratt (1987) looked at the school experience of persistent truants coming before the courts, they found, perhaps surprisingly, that the great majority of them liked most of their teachers, most lessons and had few difficulties in relationships, although like David Galloway, they did find that these persistent absentees tended to come from poor families in which there was a very high incidence of unemployment.

4.34   In fact, student accounts do more to remind us of the diversity of explanations for truancy than do some academic texts seeking for simplicity and economy of truth. We also discover that issues are often seriously considered, but that, like those of any other group, the explanations given by students are sometimes inconsistent or are used to defend personal interests.

4.35   If you are trying to understand why students absent themselves from a particular school, you might wish to focus on that school and the issues revealed by those with a special knowledge of that institution. Students, themselves, would be the group with most detailed knowledge of the reasons for their own actions. Edith Le Riche tried to capitalize on this knowledge in her study of truancy by returning to the school at which she had taught on Merseyside. She concentrated on girl students since she felt this redressed a concentration in the literature on boys. After talking to the students and their families and teachers she, too, related persistent absenteeism to the 'hopelessness and powerlessness' in an area of high unemployment and concluded 'it really is a wonder that there is not much more truancy' (Le Riche, 1988, p. 79). The students at

36

the school came up with a wide range of reasons when they wrote about truancy for her:

> Truancy is mostly caused by people hating school and the teachers. It is also caused by what you call your best mates. If your mate wants to truant and she's got no-one to go with her she will ask you and you won't say 'no I am not going' because you are scared she might call you a chicken. Sometimes truancy is caused by boredom or problems at home or with the family.
>
> (Caroline in Le Riche, 1988, p. 66)

4.36   Cynthia felt that she 'would have loved to miss a lesson of this, or a lesson of that' but that she hadn't truanted 'because I am a coward and couldn't face being found out' (Le Riche, 1988, p. 72). Julie explained why she 'sagged' (the local word for truanted) in the following way:

> I don't like school and I sag quite often. I am in a top band class and I sometimes get people telling me that I would like it better in middle and bottom band because you have a laugh.
>
> I would like to do well in school but I feel as if there is something telling me that its not worth it because of the unemployment situation here in Liverpool. When I am in school I feel as if I am in prison, you've only got to walk on the wrong side of the corridor and your teacher's on your back.
>
> If I have a problem at home I often won't go to school because I know I will end up getting told off by a teacher and then I will let out all my bad feelings. If I have a bad day (all lessons I don't like) I often sag then as well…
>
> Sometimes when I am in class and the teacher say's something I don't understand I won't put my hand up because I feel embarresed specially if all my mates have understood.
>
> When I leave I want to do secretarel work, but because of the class I am in I can't, same as in childcare I like being with children but I can't do that neither only bottom and middle band can. I think that this is wrong because I know many more people who feel the same way as I do.
>
> (Julie in Le Riche, 1988, pp. 73–4)

Activity 4   Reflecting on school attendance

Appendix 1 is a conversation between Felicity Armstrong and Nigel H, a British West Indian who, at 22, runs his own successful plumbing business. Felicity has known Nigel and his family since he was eight and explores with him some of the problems he encountered at school and in obtaining qualifications subsequently. Read the appendix now and consider how well Nigel fits into any simple categorization and explanation for his 'truancy'.

> To solve or cut down truancy we need a more consumer-fixed curriculum, the return of school attendance officers, whose salaries are adjusted according to their schools' attendance record, and the quick and heavy fining in special courts of parents who condone their children's truancy.
>
> (Rhodes Boyson, *The Times*, 5 August 1991)

4.37   Our responses to truancy depend on how we define it, the extent to which we see it as a problem, what we see as producing it and the way we connect it to other difficulties inside and outside school. Legal responses place the main onus for school attendance on parents, though the threat of incarceration in 'care' has been a potent direct weapon against some students in the past. The 'truancy industry' to which I alluded earlier generally focuses on the individual absentee. Education welfare officers are the lynchpins of the industry and have seen their role as oscillating between 'care' and 'control', though the way they characterize this role does not always coincide with the way their clients see it. Students and their parents may see any intervention by education welfare officers as an attempt at control. While individual education welfare officers may wish to examine the way school curricula contribute to truancy, their training, status and position as employees of the education service make it difficult for them to challenge the perception schools have of the 'problem'.

4.38   That there may be a politically expedient response to truancy does not, of course, affect only education welfare officers. It may affect, consciously or unconsciously, any group looking over their shoulders at the expectations of those with power over them. It may be a determining factor in the way political parties frame their policies in an attempt to be seen, for example, as strong advocates of law and order.

4.39   The recommendations of the Elton Report on truancy are interesting in this respect. Near the beginning of the report the recommendations on the various areas covered by the report are grouped together. Under 'Attendance', the Report made the following recommendations:

- Headteachers and teachers should make full use of education welfare officers to maximise attendance.

- Senior school staff should carry out frequent random attendance checks on individual lessons.

- Governors should obtain regular reports on attendance, including internal truancy, with a view to encouraging and supporting action by the school.

- All LEAs should regularly gather data on attendance at their schools and should use this information to plan the development of their resources in the most effective ways to improve attendance.

- Those designing school-based computerised information systems should take account of the possibilities of including programmes for monitoring attendance in them.

- All LEAs should maintain adequate numbers of education welfare officers to ensure that cases of unjustified absence can be followed up systematically and promptly.

- LEAs and chief officers of police should jointly consider the use of 'truancy sweeps' as a means of maximising school attendance …

(DES, 1989a, pp. 42, 44)

4.40 However, in the body of the report under the heading 'Action at school level', the first three points make a connection between the school curriculum and truancy and shift the explanation for truancy away from the failings of children and their parents:

We believe that an important first step is to reject the idea that unjustified absence can be treated as in any way helpful to schools. Heads and teachers should therefore recognise the potentially unsettling effects of any absence, and particularly of unjustified absence, on the atmosphere of schools and on pupils' behaviour. They should also recognise that the quality of a school's atmosphere and curriculum is an important factor in encouraging regular attendance.

We suggest that schools should develop positive strategies for receiving back frequent absentees. Such strategies should have two objectives. The first should be to help absentees catch up with the work that they have missed. The second should be to minimise the negative effects of this catching up process on other pupils.

Since lower achieving fourth and fifth year pupils in secondary schools have the highest rates of absence, we believe that the kind of 'alternative curriculum' approaches designed for this group which we refer to in chapter four may be particularly important in encouraging their attendance. So may work experience, compacts with employers and records of achievement, which we discuss in chapter six.

(DES, 1989a, pp. 166–7)

Why didn't these ideas find their way into the list of major recommendations?

TRUANCY AND THE LAW

4.41 In defining truancy in relation to compulsory education, I mentioned the duties and liability for prosecution of parents and how the 1989 Children Act had reduced the possibility of children being taken into care solely because of non-attendance at school. This finally stopped an approach to truancy adopted systematically in Leeds (though used elsewhere), known as the 'Leeds adjournment system' (Brown *et al.*, 1990). The practice in Leeds had raised considerable controversy because it encouraged early referral to the juvenile court and used the threat of a care or a supervision order to try to push young people into line. They were given a stay of execution of the order by having the care proceedings adjourned to see if attendance improved. The architects of this system claimed that it reduced school absence and delinquency (Brown *et al.*, 1990). Its critics argued that efforts might have been better spent working in conciliatory fashion with parents and schools. For Neville Harris, the approach aggravated the law's defect of concentrating only on the failure of parents. He argued that attendance at school was 'unlikely to achieve very much … where the child is unwilling to learn' (Harris, 1989, p. 23). The advocates of the Leeds system argue in turn that schools cannot interest students in the curriculum if they are not in school.

4.42 The government's response to some of the recommendations about truancy raised in the Elton Report and elsewhere was to issue new guidelines in August 1991 requiring all schools to distinguish between authorized and unauthorized absence from school and to keep statistics on unauthorized absences (DES, 1991). Provision was made in the 1991 Criminal Justice Act for parents to be fined up to £1000 if their children truanted. From August 1992 schools' statistics on unauthorized absences are to be published in prospectuses and annual reports. This is required of independent day schools but not independent boarding schools, presumably because the government believes that the surveillance at such schools is sufficient to prevent truancy. Michael Fallon, schools minister, saw the publication of figures as providing an incentive for schools to attract parents: 'Schools will have more incentive to do more about truancy because attendance rates will be published … Parents will then be able to compare truancy rates as one of the factors they consider in their choice of schools' (*Independent*, 16 January 1991).

4.43 The government urged the implementation of some but not all the Elton recommendations, including register spot checks, computerized attendance records and truancy sweeps. However, the idea of a local authority-wide policy initiative is undermined by the distribution to schools, in some local authorities, of some of the money to buy in education welfare services if they feel they need them. As we have seen, the Elton Report recommended that LEAs should maintain adequate numbers of education welfare officers. Are the authorities that devolve funds for them, failing to obey the law requiring them to enforce attendance at school? How will the education welfare officers be able to conduct their 'education supervision orders' if they cannot guarantee the continuity of their jobs? And are the government, in encouraging the devolution of funds, also encouraging LEAs to renege on their duties of inspection in this as in other areas of education? In 1992 new groups of private inspectors are being established. Can the *ad hoc* inspection teams that will bid for inspection contracts take over the legal duties of local government?

The change in name of truancy officers from school attendance officers to education welfare officers has hastened the decline in attendance. The school attendance officer knew what he [sic] had to do: to take the children into school. The education welfare officer often became a half-baked psychologist discussing pupils' real or imagined social, family and even sexual problems, instead of frog-marching them back in to school ...

(Rhodes Boyson, The Times, 5 August 1991)

4.44   Whatever else may be the merits of Rhodes Boyson's arguments, he is mistaken in believing that attendance has been in decline. Education welfare services operate with much the same overall levels of truancy as they did many years ago despite the successive raising of the school-leaving age.

4.45   One might have thought that a minimum number of education welfare officers was obligatory under the law but there are vast variations in the level of provision. The Elton Report quoted levels varying from one to 500 students in some areas to one to 8,500 in others (DES, 1989a, p. 169).

4.46   School attendance officers or 'school board men' came into existence with the advent of compulsory education. They were recruited from retired police and military personnel and exercised a punitive, authoritarian role in forcibly returning children to school (Local Government Training Board, 1973, para. 10) though even in those early days they were involved in providing 'food, fuel and clothing to [some] poor families' (Wardhaugh, 1990, p. 737). The switch in name to education welfare officer came after the 1944 Education Act.

4.47   Although there have been increasing numbers of trained social workers and teachers working as education welfare officers, their pay has lagged way behind either of these groups. There are no national pay scales and individual local authorities make their own agreements.

4.48   The history of the education welfare service is characterized by two major and connected themes concerned with the balance between 'controlling' and 'caring' functions and the development of professional status. Arguments for improving professional status have depended, largely, on the idea that education welfare officers perform a complex social-work role. The conflict between the functions of control and caring is mirrored by the wider battle for the control of the education welfare services between education and social service departments, similar to the disputes about under-five care which you encountered in the case study of Strathclyde in Unit 5. Writing in 1987, Eric Blyth and Judith Milner argue that 'non-attendance at school has become the single most contentious issue between social services and education departments' (Blyth and Milner, 1987, p. 155).

4.49   In 1968 the Seebohm enquiry into local authority social services recommended that education welfare services should be integrated into social services departments (DHSS, 1968). A few authorities made the change, but by and large the service remained firmly within education. Education consolidated its position over attendance with the 1969 Children and Young Persons Act which gave it powers to institute care proceedings and present social services departments with candidates for their children's homes. Yet the 1973 Ralphs Report on the training of education welfare officers continued the emphasis on 'caring' and noted that local authorities increasingly rejected 'authoritarian methods of securing attendance' (Local Government Training Board, 1973). However, a decade later the Conservative Party manifesto signalled a change of rhetoric with its pledge to 'switch the emphasis of the education welfare service back to school attendance' (quoted in Blyth and Milner, 1987, p. 158). These sentiments were repeated in DES Circular 2/86 which offered local authorities guidance on 'school attendance and education welfare services'. Subsequently, Circular 11/91 was quite specific that 'the EWS is the attendance enforcement arm of most LEAs'. It suggested that early recourse to the courts might be the best way to achieve results:

> In many cases of unauthorised absence an early and firm approach to the parents may bring a prompt and sustained improvement. Some authorities have found early prosecution of parents to be particularly effective, not only in relation to the individual child, but also as a signal to other parents that such conduct will not be accepted.
>
> (DES, 1991, Appendix 1)

4.50   In practice, however, while the balance may shift, education welfare officers retain a range of attitudes, as Julia Wardhaugh's study revealed. Her interviewees varied in their willingness to bring prosecutions from one a week to 'occasionally through the year'.

EWO 1 With the good families the threat of a court case is enough, it scares them and encourages a more positive attitude towards education. With others, of course, they don't care, they're in court every week anyway ... I wouldn't want to make too many home visits, become too familiar with the families as this would take away the deterrent effect of my visits. That would be no good if I'm to be a prosecuting machine.

EWO 2 I like to get to know the families, understand their problems. I'd only prosecute as a very last resort, after I'd tried everything else. I see myself as someone who cares for the families, not just someone who knocks on doors.

(Wardhaugh, 1991, p. 753–4)

4.51   In my local area, as in many other areas, education welfare officers are attached to a secondary school and the primary schools which feed most children to it. A new conflict is emerging between welfare officers and teachers over the increase in exclusions of pupils, since such non-attendance, however justified, is directly produced by schools. As my informant explained:

We're very much involved in exclusions. If a child is out of school our job is to work with the local authority school support officer to get them back. We are the link with the family. It does happen that we get pupils back into school and then they are excluded. We get very cross because I believe that youngsters know how to work the system because if they are excluded they are legitimately out.

(Education welfare officer, 1992, personal communication)

4.52   Education welfare officers' aims should be the same for all students who are out of school, whether excluded or truanting: they should ensure that more students are benefiting from education. Central government, LEAs and schools urgently need to rethink policies on exclusion and to make the link between these policies and those on truancy.

SUMMARY AND CONCLUSION

4.53   In this section I have reviewed some approaches to truancy and have argued for a careful analysis of possible causes within schools, taking account of the reasons given for absence by students and their families, rather than searching for a simple general explanation of truancy. I have suggested that truancy can be defined in relation to the duties of parents to ensure that their children are appropriately educated and of education authorities to ensure that this happens. Truancy, then, is all illegal absence from school. School phobia is a 'medical or unavoidable cause' of school absence, and is to be distinguished from truancy, though students experiencing similar difficulties may be assigned to different categories. Truancy may be condoned by parents and also by some schools. Absence from school would still be a problem for parents and schools if schooling were voluntary.

4.54   The numbers of students absent from schools has remained remarkably stable over the years despite the raising of the school-leaving age. However, absence increases with age and large numbers of students in the final years of compulsory schooling engage in selective truancy.

4.55   Students truant from school for many reasons: because they dislike school or feel it is irrelevant and that it does not add to their employment prospects, or because on a particular occasion they have better things to do. Persistent, long-term truancy is associated with acute material family hardship. Some children who truant do come from uncaring homes but most who truant do not.

4.56   Variations in truancy rates between schools and for different age groups provide strong evidence that schools, through improvements to curricula and culture, can make a large difference to attendance patterns.

4.57   Responses to truancy have oscillated between controlling and caring policies. Up to the 1980s, the welfare of students was increasingly emphasized in discussions of interventions, though subsequently the government has stressed punishment for parents and a direct attack on school attendance. It has also argued that parents' knowledge of truancy rates will exert pressure on schools to reduce them. The Elton Report discussed a range of responses to truancy, involving both curriculum development and the close surveillance of students, but stressed the latter (DES, 1989a).

4.58   The education welfare service has vacillated uneasily between education and social work though without the professional status of either. It retains major responsibility for dealing with truants with changed powers of 'supervision' of students under the 1989 Children Act. However, the services are under threat from devolution of centrally held budgets to the schools.

4.58   The duty placed on parents by the 1944 Education Act is to ensure education for their children rather than attendance at school yet most of the effort and writing that surrounds truancy is preoccupied with attendance. This course assumes that the provision of an appropriate education for the diversity of students is the starting point for attempts to reduce difficulties in learning. It should also be the starting point for the reduction of truancy.

5   ABUSING POWER

CALIBAN I'll kiss thy foot. I'll swear myself thy subject.

STEPHANO Come on, down and swear.

TRINCULO I shall laugh myself to death at this puppyheaded monster. A most scurvy monster! I could find in my heart to beat him –

(Shakespeare, *The Tempest*, 1611 Oxford edition, p. 150)

5.1   What is it about the power relationship between Caliban and his captors that produces such denigration and violence? In this section I will look at the excesses and abuses of power among students, among teachers and students and among schoolworkers themselves. While bullying is usually seen as something school students do to one another, I will argue, that adults commonly bully other adults as well as children, where in extreme cases it may take the form of child abuse. I will suggest that efforts at curbing it will have limited success until its roots in the adult world are exposed. I will ask whether sexual and racial harassment in schools can be seen as forms of bullying. Until the late 1980s, corporal punishment was a common feature of life in schools in the UK. Was it a reasonable form of control and discipline? I will chart the abolition of corporal punishment in state schools and the reactions to, and implications of, the abolition. I will end the section by asking what forms of control are available to teachers to exercise their responsibilities and preserve their rights and those of their students.

5.2   In the UK bullying in schools received growing attention from the late 1980s (Lane and Tattum, 1989; Skinner, 1992). It is a perennial feature of school life but following progress made in combating bullying in Scandinavia, particularly Norway, academics and the media turned their attention to it closer to home. It has been defined as involving *'persistent, deliberate, unprovoked, physical or psychological harm by a more powerful child or young person or group, against a weaker child or group'* (Smith, 1991). However, I cannot see a good reason to exclude single instances from the definition. I think we should be cautious, too, about the notion of provocation. Presumably the reaction must be justified by the initial action. One secondary school boy was regarded as a nuisance by his teachers and classmates. For some time, until the teacher intervened following complaints from some parents, a group of boys had been attacking him physically saying how much they loathed him. They would have said they were provoked by his behaviour and even his year tutor offered the suggestion that he was 'an inadequate' as part justification for the assaults. It seemed to me that this went some way to asserting the acceptability of bullying in the school.

5.3   Delwyn Tattum and Graham Herbert offer a broader definition. In *Bullying: a positive response* (Tattum and Herbert, 1990) they define bullying as 'the wilful, conscious desire to hurt, threaten or frighten someone' (p. 3). This definition attributes bullying to desires as well as behaviour and I think this is mistaken. Should I be held responsible for my desires? I would substitute 'attempt' for 'desire' here. How would you define it?

Activity 5   How much bullying goes on in comprehensive schools? –

Colin Yates and Peter Smith investigated the extent of bullying in two schools in England in an attempt to compare these with Norwegian investigations. Their findings are reported in 'Bullying in two English comprehensive schools', Chapter 20 in Reader 1, which you should now read.

- Any assessment of the extent of bullying depends on the precise way it is measured. How is bullying defined both for bullies and victims? Is there anything included in the definition that you think should be omitted? Is there any behaviour excluded from this definition that should be included?

- Think about the way the findings are reported. Is this done clearly?

- Think about the findings. Do any of them surprise you? Do they match what you already know about bullying? What particular findings would you like to investigate further?

- Think about the generalizations that are made from the findings. What do reports from two English schools in one city tell us about the rest of that city, the rest of England or the rest of the United Kingdom? What do the Norwegian results tell us about the rest of Scandinavia?

5.4 The definition of bullying that is used in the chapter included name-calling and repeated teasing, as well as physical constraint and assault; these take place when it is 'difficult for the young person being bullied to defend himself or herself' (p. 225–6). There is another aspect of bullying that does not seem to be included here, though it may apply more to primary pupils and to girls in particular. It is familiar to me from the stories of pupils at local primary schools and is graphically and, I believe, authentically portrayed in Margaret Atwood's *Cat's Eye*. In that book Elaine persists in regarding Cordelia as her best friend despite the regular humiliation and emotional torture meted out by Cordelia herself or by her deputies in their closed circle of friends. Elaine is unable to walk away from the group because life beyond it seems unthinkable. Her mother and Cordelia's mother both know about it but do nothing; the former in the mistaken belief that·intervention will make matters worse; the latter because she colludes in the view that Elaine, child of an ungodly family, somehow deserves her treatment. As she remembers what happened, Elaine imagines that her mother must have thought that these were small events taking place between small 'cute' girls. But as she remarks, Cordelia and the others were 'life-sized' to her. Elaine only begins to emerge from her emotional imprisonment when, as a consequence of having her hat thrown 'playfully' into a gully, she is almost frozen to death. I have included an extract from the book below. Some of you will have memories of similar types of bullying from your schooldays, others may be in similar situations now, at work or at home:

> On the window-ledge beside mine, Cordelia and Grace and Carol are sitting, jammed in together, whispering and giggling. I have to sit on a window-ledge by myself because they aren't speaking to me. It's something I said wrong, but I don't know what it is because they won't tell me. Cordelia says it will be better for me to think back over everything I've said today and try to pick out the wrong thing. That way I will learn not to say such a thing again. When I've guessed the right answer, then they will speak to me again. All of this is for my own good, because they are my best friends and they want to help me improve. So this is what I'm thinking about as the pipe band goes past in sodden fur hats, and the drum majorettes with their bare wet legs and red smiles and dripping hair: what did I say wrong? I can't remember having said anything different from what I would ordinarily say.
>
> My father walks into the room, wearing his white lab coat. He's working in another part of the building, but he's come in to check on us. 'Enjoying the parade, girls?' he says.

'Oh yes, thank you,' Carol says, and giggles. Grace says, 'Yes, thank you.' I say nothing. Cordelia gets down off her windowsill and slides up on mine, sitting close beside me.

'We're enjoying it extremely, thank you very much,' she says in her voice for adults. My parents think she has beautiful manners. She puts an arm around me, gives me a little squeeze, a squeeze of complicity, of instruction. Everything will be all right as long as I sit still, say nothing and reveal nothing. I will be saved then, I will be acceptable once more. I smile, tremulous with relief, with gratitude.

But as soon as my father is out of the room Cordelia turns to face me. Her expression is sad rather than angry. She shakes her head. 'How could you?' she says. 'How could you be so impolite? You didn't even answer him. You know what this means, don't you? I'm afraid you'll have to be punished. What do you have to say for yourself?' And I have nothing to say.

I'm standing outside the closed door of Cordelia's room. Cordelia, Grace and Carol are inside. They're having a meeting. The meeting is about me. I am just not measuring up, although they are giving me every chance. I will have to do better. But better at what?

Perdie and Mirrie [Cordelia's sisters] come up the stairs, along the hall, in their armour of being older. I long to be as old as they are. They're the only people who have any real power over Cordelia, that I can see. I think of them as my allies; or I think they would be my allies if they only knew. Knew what? Even to myself I am mute.

(Atwood, 1988, p. 116–8)

If, at the time, Elaine could not even tell herself about her ordeal, how would she respond to a researcher's questions about bullying?

5.5 When I read Colin Yates' and Peter Smith's chapter, I found that its main messages were clear by the end but that at times I had been overwhelmed by the tables and numbers. I was confused too by switching from percentages to actual numbers and by the way percentages of a subgroup of the total were sometimes – and I could not grasp immediately how serious a problem this implied. Did you have any similar reactions?

5.6 The main things that struck me about the findings, apart from the prevalence of the problem were that it largely went undetected and that there were important gender differences. For example, boys were usually bullied by other boys but girls were bullied by both boys and girls. This did not surprise me given what I know about boys' attempts to exert power over boys and girls, particularly through forms of sexual harassment. But the way bullying was defined may have under-represented victimization of girls by other girls as I indicated above. A broader definition and other questions might have revealed more bullying of boys by girls, too. A possible way of investigating this further would be to ask a preliminary question like, 'When girls bully boys what form does this take?' This could be followed up with more precise questions about incidence.

5.7   The authors report that almost as many students said they had been bullied 'at least now and then' outside school as inside school. They set this finding against the Norwegian study by Olweus (1989) which argues that 'the school is, no doubt, where most of the bullying occurs'. Without arguing about the precise figures, I am sure that a considerable amount of bullying is between siblings, particularly of younger children by older brothers or sisters. Similarly the definition of bullying used in the reader chapter excludes bullying of children by adults, whether in school or out of school. I think this narrowing of the phenomenon of bullying makes it harder to explain and reduce.

5.8   Since this chapter was written, Peter Smith (1991) has added further qualifications to the findings. In a later paper he noted how early figures suggesting that bullying in some English Schools were far in excess of the figures reported by Norway prompted a report in the *Guardian* that 'Britain is the bullying capital of Europe' (*Guardian*, 28 September 1989). He pointed out the misleading nature of such claims, which are based on limited samples of schools, and argued that the available evidence suggests bullying in schools in Norway and Scotland (Mellor, 1990) may be relatively low while the figures emerging from England, Spain and Ireland are substantially higher.

Intervening in bullying

5.9   Since attention has been focused on bullying in school many suggestions have been made about how it can be reduced. All approaches start with persuading staff and students in schools that there is a problem and that instances of bullying need to be brought to the notice of responsible adults. Drama has been used to great effect as a way of raising the issue and we have devoted one of our television programmes to the reactions of teachers and students to a play about bullying written and performed by the Neti Neti theatre company. This company perform in English, Bengali and Sign-supported English, using deaf and hearing actors. The play is called *Only Playing, Miss!* (Casdagli *et al.*, 1990) and was devised through a series of workshops with students at the Guildhall School for Music and Drama and was built around their own experiences of bullying at school, both as bullies and victims. The play itself lasts for 50 minutes but we were only able to afford to use five minutes of the drama because of a broadcasting agreement with the actors' union, Equity, which required that all televised drama is paid for at West End of London rates.

5.10   The performance took place at Fortismere School in Haringey, a comprehensive school with a department for deaf and partially hearing students. We interspersed extracts from the play with comments from the cast, teachers and students and recorded part of a workshop put on by the theatre company with some of the students who had watched the play. This reversed the order in which Neti Neti prefer to work, since they normally start with workshops so that students are familiar with exploring the roles of bully, victim, friend, observer, teacher and parent. The last part of the programme is a studio discussion about the intervention in the school, the way it is portrayed on film and about bullying more generally.

Activity 6 TV6 Danger, Children at Play

If possible watch TV6 at this point. The short extracts of the play that we have been able to show only give a glimpse of the power of the play itself. It may help you to view the play and understand the reactions to it if I give a character list and the part each character plays in the story.

Eugene: He is the main (but not the only) victim in the play. He is distressed by the recent death of his father and has written a poem about the death. His mother is distressed, too, and he does not feel he can burden her with the problems he has at school.

Becky: Initially she joins in with the girls who tease Eugene about his poem but she quickly draws back. She is a friend of Eugene but also of Rant, the main (but not the only) bully in the play. She tells Rant about the poem and he snatches it from her. She finds herself teased by Sam because of her support for and friendship with Eugene. Eventually, with Hashi, she tells their form tutor.

Sam: With the other girls she discovers the poem in our first extract. She reads it mockingly and begins Eugene's torment.

Hashi: A friend of Becky and Sam. She supports Becky in telling their form tutor about the bullying.

Mr Wallace: He is the PE teacher, who has little patience with the emotional difficulties of students and particularly with boys who write poems. When he realises about the bullying he does nothing about it: 'Grow up, lad. It's a tough world out there boy. Now pull yourself together' (Casdagli *et al.*, 1990, p. 53).

David Rant (called Rant in the play): He leads the brutal bullying of Eugene. He has troubles of his own which he does not face up to himself and which he hides from his schoolmates. His mother has recently left home. He has a stormy relationship with his father and is hit by him.

Mark Cheeseman (known as Cheesey in the play): He is the willing sidekick of Rant and his accomplice in the violence.

Jo: He is a friend of Eugene who says he must do something about the bullying and is willing to stand up for him.

Mrs Richards: She is the form tutor. She is sympathetic to Eugene and once she hears about it, she is determined that the bullying should stop.

If possible, watch the programme with others so that you can pool your responses. Make a note of the points you want to raise as you watch the programme and as soon as it is finished. You may wish to reflect on your own experience of bullying, as a bully or a victim, at school or elsewhere. Perhaps there are young people you know well who are having similar problems.

In a short programme some issues are glossed over. There is, for example, a disagreement about whether deaf students are more likely to experience bullying than other students. There is a suggestion that sexual harassment is not a form of bullying. You might consider the reactions of the teachers. Can they exert their power in order to stop bullying without providing models for the abuse of power that constitutes bullying? I will take up these and other issues when you have viewed the programme.

5.11 *Only Playing, Miss!* had a powerful effect on its audience. One boy was sobbing at the end because it reminded him of 'so many things that had happened to him'. Others put their heads in their laps, a common reaction according to the director, from those who bully. There was rapt attention throughout the performance, stunned silence for a moment when it finished and then prolonged applause.

5.12 The teachers felt that the play had successfully made staff aware of the problems of bullying and brought it out in the open for students too. One teacher remarked that the action was convincing but that there should be such a clear reason for bullying was unusual: 'Quite often there isn't a reason particularly. It's just that the bully tends to want to make themselves powerful.' A child remarked that everybody in the play 'was bullied except Sam and Hashi'. She was referring to the students though, as I have suggested, teachers can be victimized, too, both by students and other teachers. (The actor playing Mrs Richards hopes that the strength she puts into the character will help teachers since 'I've known some of my schoolteachers were bullied'.) In the full-length play there is a scene at Sam's slumber party where Becky is teased unpleasantly about her relationship with Eugene and subsequently this incident is magnified and spread around the class:

> BECKY: He's nice to you and you're so horrible to him.
>
> (*Sam laughs with disbelief*)
>
> SAM: *Nice!* Oh Becky, Becky, tell us what you like about him best. Is it his poetry? Or his clothes? Or the way he cries?
>
> (Casdagli *et al.*, 1990, p. 57)

5.13 Individual teachers gave very different reactions to some aspects of the play. One teacher felt that in the last twenty years she hadn't met a teacher with the macho insensitivity of the PE teacher. Another thought him commonplace and as reflecting some aspects of herself at times. There were differing views about 'Mrs Richards'. Was she right to react so fiercely, without delving into the reasons for the bullying? Could she have made herself equally clear and determined without shouting? What purpose did the shouting serve? If it was an unpremeditated expression of anger, is it right for teachers to lose control in order to gain control in this way? And what would happen next? One teacher alluded to the experience of making a determined statement to students which it is then difficult to follow through.

5.14   Barbara Maines and George Robinson have written an article critical of the kind of approach taken by 'Mrs Richards' called 'Don't beat the bullies' (Maines and Robinson, 1991). They argue that 'You will not do this' is a mistaken strategy and, following the work of Pikas (1989), call for the bully to be drawn into a shared moral network of 'common concern'. They stress in the training they offer schools that bullying is not 'abnormal' and that bullies should not be punished but that following an incident all those involved or who know about the bullying should be drawn into discussions which make the victim's hurt clear, bring the bullying out into the open and minimize the possibility of retaliation for 'telling'.

The use of sign

5.15   The studio discussion was arranged to allow some of the issues a greater airing and because I was concerned about the way signing was represented in the film. The actors used Sign-supported English throughout the performance and this made it relatively accessible to deaf students. The use of sign contributed to the integrity of a play for a multilingual audience performed by deaf and hearing actors. (The actors playing Becky and Mrs Richards were both deaf.) When I saw the rushes of the day's filming I was taken aback to discover that the camera had been so tight up to the performers that some signs were disappearing off the edge of the screen. This seemed to me to be discourteous to the spirit of the play and to any deaf viewers. The justification from colleagues was that the drama demanded close-ups and that these would inevitably cut out the sign. How then, I wondered, could one film a drama performed only in British Sign Language? The dispute was resolved by allowing feedback on this aspect of the film. Carole Tweedy, who is involved in another theatre group called Co-Sign, points out that the film was edited with a hearing audience in mind. She refers to another issue about the particular form of sign in the play. Sign-supported English, in which British Sign Language signs are used simultaneously with the main words of English, was used. But for full access for deaf people to the nuances of language it might be argued that the performance would have to be in British Sign Language itself though it then could not be in English simultaneously. Carole Tweedy suggests that it all depends on the audience.

Bullying and disability

5.16   Are deaf students particularly prone to being bullied? Two teachers of the deaf in the programme expressed different views. The teacher in charge of the department for deaf students in the school suggested that they were and told me that they had transferred to Fortismere School because of their experiences of bullying in a previous school, although other teachers who I spoke to in her department did not feel this was the case. Another teacher, in the studio discussion, implies that they are like other students in this respect. Early in the programme one of the students in the audience remarks that the death of a parent creates a vulnerability in Eugene which is then exploited. Penny Casdagli, the director, expands this notion when she argues that differences between students are picked on and that the use of three languages in the drama symbolizes the acceptance of difference. A difference, it might be argued, is turned into a vulnerability through the belief and assertion that there is a normality which is the only guarantee of acceptance. Deafness in students may provide the opportunity for someone to discomfort them and exert power over them. There are characteristics in all students that can be used in similar ways, but in our society, just as many people have to contend with racism by virtue of being black, others face disablism. The notions of normality on which such attitudes are built thrive outside schools and it would be surprising if they did not surface within them. The special twist in the education of the deaf is that some of those who contribute most to defining deafness as an abnormality are educators of the deaf, who, as I suggested in Unit 10 (para. 5.47) may argue for a narrow view of normalization. Does this attitude and the behaviour it promotes itself constitute bullying?

Believing what young people say?

5.17   In 1991 the *Observer* published an account of alleged bullying of Rebecca, a girl with cerebral palsy, because she was not made in the image of a perfect member of a school band. The steel band had a considerable reputation and according to the report, 'three girls in the band plus an adult helper caused her great unhappiness by sarcasm and whispering against her: they made it clear that they didn't want her in the band or think she should be there' (*Observer*, 28 April 1991). The story is instructive because of the subtle nature of the bullying it involved and the fact that neither she nor her parents were able to persuade the teacher in charge of the band, or the headteacher, that any bullying was taking place. As Rebecca commented, 'You expect a teacher to believe pupils if they say they're being bullied, to listen to both sides and sort it out. No one would do that for me.'

5.18   In May 1992, in England, a young girl committed suicide and left a note saying that she was killing herself because she was bullied at the school. The coroner was persuaded by the view of the police that she had not been bullied but that the pressure of GCSE work had been exacerbated by high parental expectations. Many would argue that we cannot hope to do anything about bullying until we trust what young people tell us, make ourselves available and can be trusted to receive their confidence.

Bullying and harassment, one problem or two?

5.19   Children and young people may truant as a result of bullying. Bullying and harassment which start off with words can lead to violence and, in extreme cases, to suicide or murder. Members of some groups, which together make up the majority of people in society, grow up knowing that they may be attacked or even killed, simply by virtue of their membership of that group. This applies to women, black people and gay people but may include other groups as new hatreds and fears are projected their way. It has become customary to talk of harassment when a person is denigrated or attacked because of their membership of a particular group. Are sexual and racial harassment forms of bullying? Perhaps the question is trivial since it is more important to recognize that they occur and require intervention than to worry over much about definitions. And of course we have the freedom to define them as we wish. But is it wise to define harassment as a form of bullying? Elinor Kelly (1991) has drawn attention to the problems that can arise in separating bullying and racial and sexual harassment as separate specializations: 'This fragmentation generates problems for pupils, parents, teachers and school support services who cannot then deal with the 'whole' experience of pupils because they are categorised as black *or* white, female *or* male, able-bodied *or* disabled' (Kelly, 1991, p. 17).

5.20   Nevertheless, Elinor Kelly does want to maintain the distinction between bullying and harassment in its various guises; 'where the victims … are not heard because their tormentors appeal to norms and values in justifying their behaviour' (p. 19). My feeling is that if we attempt to define bullying to exclude harassment we end up with a very clumsy definition. But we do have to be scrupulously aware of the problems raised by different forms of bullying. A sexual assault by a boy on a girl raises the need to counter particular behaviour and attitudes to all girls. A hurtful remark about the wearing of glasses may not result in the same wounding of a child's identity as remarks about the colour of their skin or their Irish nationality.

Sexual harassment

5.21   Sexual harassment involves the imposition of unwanted sexual remarks or contact. Carrie Herbert states in TV6 that sexual harassment is not a form of bullying. She argues that sexual harassment can only be perpetrated by boys and men and that it differs from bullying, too, in that it often passes for 'normal male behaviour'. Everyone, she suggests, can put a label to bullying and recognize that it is wrong. Is it wise to distinguish sexual harassment from bullying in this way? I would argue that, on the contrary, bullying can occur in front of some people without them recognizing what is happening or how hurtful it is. Carrie Herbert has argued elsewhere that 'sexual harassment is dependent on the combined effect of two forms of power: individual (or personal) power, and institutional power'(Herbert, 1991, p. 12). Yet it is hard to see how this definition excludes the possibility of men and boys being harassed sexually by women or girls or by other men or boys and sexual harassment of women or girls by other women or girls. We can recognize that sexual harassment is primarily a problem for women and girls because of male power and intimidation, without excluding men and boys from the possibility of being sexually harassed. Near the start of her book, Carrie Herbert gives an example of 'elusive sexual harassment':

A woman teacher was taking a 5 year old boy to the sick room because he was not feeling well. He was holding her hand. As they passed the headteacher's office the head spoke to the little boy, while ignoring the teacher. He said, 'You had better enjoy holding that lady's hand, Johnny, because when you are as old as me you won't be allowed to.' I am sure that for some people this will be regarded as an innocuous remark, but I label it sexual harassment.

(Herbert, 1991, Introduction)

But in imputing sexuality to the action of the boy isn't this 'elusive sexual harassment' of the child too?

Sexist abuse

5.22   I would regard sexist abuse, in which a person's gender is devalued or denigrated, as a form of bullying too. It takes blatant as well as more subtle forms. It is prevalent in schools and in the literature and the media used in schools. I have been struck by the poor choice of school plays at some schools in which girls are viewed as adjuncts to heroic and successful men. At a local school my elder daughter attended, the play one year was *How to Succeed in Business Without Really Trying*, a tale of men's trips to the top watched by admiring secretaries. A few years later I watched in amazement while girls aged 13–16 at my nephew's school performed a scene from *Damn Yankees* in front of parents, teachers and friends. They were dressed in black underwear, stockings and suspenders, danced erotically and sang 'Who gets the pain when we do the mambo?'.

5.23   Afterwards I asked the drama teacher what was meant by this particular line. She did not answer that question but immediately went into a defence of the girls' costumes on the grounds that they had 'chosen them themselves'. Several of the people I asked about the performance said they had seen nothing amiss with it. Was it a celebration of female sexuality or a complex sexual harassment of the girls?

5.24   In the same play the girl playing Lola trumpeted the familiar stereotype of the means for girls to get on in the world:

> You gotta know what to say and how to say it
> You gotta know what game to play and how to play it
> You gotta stack those decks with a couple-a extra aces
>
> (*Hanky across chest in both hands*)
>
> And this queen has her aces
> In all the right places!
>
> (*Pull hanky down across body*)
>
> I've done much more than that old bore, Delilah!
> I took the curl out of the hair of a millionaire
>
> (*Hanky across behind*)

There's no trick gettin' some hick who is cool
Just a little warmer
A little talent – A little brains
(*Taps head*)
With an emphasis on the former!
(Adler and Ross, 1955)

Should we accept, without comment, songs in praise of the subordination of girls' intellectual achievement to the development of their sexual power?

Activity 7 Changing ideas in a primary school?

Now read Chapter 6 in Reader 2 by Sheila Cunnison, 'Challenging patriarchal culture through equal opportunities: an action research study in a primary school'. It describes an attempt to understand and intervene in the creation of expectations of the way girls and boys should behave and discusses the relationship between problems of behaviour, particularly of boys, and difficulties in learning. When you have read the chapter consider the following questions more closely.

- What is the relevance of this chapter to the arguments of this section?

- What are the findings on aspirations and participation reported in section 3 of the chapter?

- What do you think of the arguments about the relationship between reading difficulties and disruptive behaviour?

5.25   Sometimes the set readings may seem to interrupt the flow of the units, because they cover a range of issues only some of which seem immediately relevant. Sheila Cunnison's chapter is not concerned with dramatic examples of sexism or sexual harassment, although some are alluded to, but with the conditions which foster the emergence of such attitudes and the possibilities for countering them. She is not only concerned with the way girls may be held back by sexist attitudes but with the way these affect boys too. She raises the huge issue of the predominance of difficulties in learning among boys, perceived and actual disruption by boys and the relationship between the two. Difficulties in learning and disruption demand attention. If they predominantly involve boys then they take attention away from girls. Disruption in classrooms may provide practice in using the power of one's body and voice to dominate and determine interactions.

5.26   In section 3 of the chapter, some of the findings are not what the author expected. The girls who made the least stereotyped responses were in the classes of those teachers who were least interested in countering stereotypes. But in all the classes the dream jobs were not as clearly divided by gender as the stereotypes might lead us to suppose. The results about the way teachers divided their attention between boys and girls were clear and were related to difficulties in behaviour of the boys and different styles of contribution from girls and boys.

5.27   The thirteen weeks of paired-reading withdrawal for those with reading difficulties was said to lead to marked improvements in reading and behaviour. Sheila Cunnison suggests an explanation of the disruption in terms of frustration and boredom brought on by an inability to join in lessons because of a reading difficulty: 'It is likely that ... the acquisition of reading skills decreases frustration and boredom – both of which may result in disruption – and increases confidence and the ability to join in lessons' (Reader 2, Chapter 6, p. 97).

5.28   While, commonly, participation in lessons does depend on literacy, should means be found to maximize the participation of students irrespective of their levels of attainment and to counter measuring esteem and self-esteem in terms of attainment? The sense of being devalued creates, as I have suggested, a pool of potential disaffection. As things are, raising the educational standard of some students may facilitate their participation, but we would still need to avoid ascribing value to students according to their attainments. Tackling this latter problem may do more in the longer term to reduce the pool of the disaffected.

Racial harassment and racism

5.29   Paul Gordon has drawn together information about racial violence and harassment, including that in schools, in a report for the Runnymede Trust (Gordon, 1990). An examination of this issue forms part of another Open University course called *Race, Education and Society* (Open University, 1992) and is examined, in particular, in one of the readers for that course, *Racism and Education* (Gill, Mayor and Blair, 1992). The Commission for Racial Equality published a survey of racial harassment in schools and colleges in England, Scotland and Wales for the years 1985–7 called *Learning in Terror* (CRE, 1988). In surveying the limited amount of research they cite a study by the Scottish Ethnic Minority Research Unit. Within its sample of ethnic minority students in South Glasgow, 25 per cent had experienced damage to property, 37 per cent had experienced personal racial attacks and 100 per cent had been subject to racial abuse (CRE, 1988, p. 9). The CRE report concluded:

> The problem of racial harassment extends right through the educational system from nursery and infant schools to colleges and universities and affects pupils, students, parents and staff ... Abuse, graffiti and violence ... serve as a constant reminder of the intolerance of white society and the vulnerability of ethnic minority people ...

> The seriousness of the situation is not matched by a corresponding awareness and sense of urgency on the part of quite a number of LEAs ...

> What is needed is a redefinition of what it means to be a professional ... the true professional will be characterised by a powerful commitment to racial justice.
>
> (CRE, 1988, p. 16)

5.30   A single case, the murder of a British-Asian school student at Burnage High School in Manchester, was documented in detail by an inquiry chaired by Ian Mcdonald. The inquiry was commissioned by Manchester Council to look at racism and racial violence in Manchester schools but the report was withheld by them because it was argued that the findings might be libellous. The report was eventually published independently under the title *Murder in the Playground* (Macdonald *et al.*, 1989).

5.31   Racial fights had become common between Afro-Caribbean, Asian and white groups at Burnage High School. A particular white student, Darren Coulburn, enjoyed tormenting younger British-Asian students. Ahmed Iqbal Ullah took it upon himself to defend them and this brought him into conflict with Darren. The two fought before school on 17 September 1986. Darren pulled out a knife and stabbed Ahmed. Teachers were unaware of the first aid appropriate to a stabbing, there was a delay in calling an ambulance, and by the time he arrived at the hospital 40 minutes later Ahmed was dead.

5.32   The school had had considerable problems and there was low morale among staff and ill-feeling towards the head and deputy head, as revealed the previous year in inspections by governors and a local authority team of inspectors. The report was critical of the way the school had attempted to combat racism. For example, the senior management had set up ethnic minority advisory groups which conveyed an impression to staff, parents and students that a greater role in the school was being given to the parents of black than white students. The report argued that an appropriate anti-racist strategy was essential to combat racism in schools but that in its equal opportunities policy the school should have included the needs of white students from a largely working class area whose opportunities might be restricted. The majority of the nation's newspapers poured the findings of the report through their ideological sieve and decided that the report had blamed Ahmed's death on anti-racist teaching. They completely lost sight of the fact that Ahmed Ullah had been murdered and that racism, according to the report, had played an essential part in his killing.

THE PROBLEMS OF STUDENTS AND THE WORLD OF ADULTS

5.33   In the case of racial and sexual harassment or sexist abuse between students it ought to be transparent that they reflect values of the world of adults. Yet some people discuss bullying as if it were separate from the adult world, a phenomenon of the playground and a problem of childhood that needs to be recognized and then dealt with by ensuring that students are properly socialized into adult morality. This is the view of Golding's *Lord of the Flies*, where out of sight of adult eyes the fabric of culture breaks down. But don't the moralities of some adults include bullying as an essential feature? That the weak should go to the wall and be kicked when they get there. We create a paradigm of childhood bullying as physical assault, like that by Rant and Cheesey on Eugene, but perhaps the subtle degradation of Elaine in *Cat's Eye* provides a model closer to home, in which a private brutal reality is unacknowledged in public. And like Elaine we may find that even to ourselves 'we are mute'. As I write this I have to drag out the thought that is once more about to be buried. How can anyone think that bullying is a problem of childhood when they know what adults are willing to do to each other? How many Trinculos are there, how many Calibans?

Bullying at work

5.34   In April and May 1991 Andrea Adams presented two programmes for Radio 4 on bullying at work. The economic power which 'superiors' can wield over other employees, heightened in times of high unemployment, make bullying at work particularly insidious and difficult to escape from. The ubiquitous 'employer's reference' can haunt someone long after they have removed themselves from the immediate unpleasantness of being bullied. One of the teachers on the programme, bullied by her head, explained how, although the local authority adviser had offered to write a reference, the absence of a head's reference could brand her as a troublemaker at other schools.

> Your present employer or your last employer always has to write your reference for you. That's the problem all the way along about making any kind of fuss when you're in a school. So I've always got to give my head as a referee if I apply for another job. So he can make sure that I never work again, and in fact threatened me with that on several occasions. And I think that's one of the reasons why the staff found it hard to unite against him because heads are very powerful in that respect. They can ensure that you cannot move into another job and if you resign, that you cannot get another job. Towards the end of the bullying, when the authority was involved, I did discuss this problem with the educational adviser who said, 'Well, you can put me down as a reference. Don't put your head down, put me down and I'll write you a reference,' but by that stage the implication had been made by him that if I continued to fight my head I'd be labelled as a troublemaker and he implied that perhaps he saw me as a troublemaker ... If you apply for a job and you don't give the head of your school that you're working at as a referee and you give your adviser instead, any head is going to know there's something very odd going on and probably the reason is that you're having some kind of argument with your head and he'll draw his own conclusions.

5.35   Andrea Adams included five case studies in the programme from the many she had examined. A trainee nurse told of the way she was tormented by management because of her bleached cropped hair, of the illness and nervousness the bullying caused and how she eventually sought and gained support from the Royal College of Nursing. They told the staff at her hospital to concentrate on criteria relevant to the job but could not affect the power of her employers to stop her working in the hospital. A bank employee told how a particular manager created a regime where, with 'henchmen', he was able to bully large numbers of employees until a comprehensive dossier was taken to the union and the bank was forced to do something about it. At the start she could not believe what was happening:

> You don't think of it in respectable places of work … It's not physical, it's everything but … It was a long time before it showed itself as actual bullying, that you could attach that label to it … It's so personal, so that a lot of what happened you didn't tell anyone about.

5.36 A full-time parish worker argued that bullying of parish workers and curates by vicars was commonplace in a 'feudally' organized Church of England.

> We're all a bit selfish. We tend not to notice what's happening to somebody else, and also if you're an outsider watching from your side it doesn't sound too bad, it might sound quite legitimate but it's got at that person … I don't think it's recognized. Certainly not as a major problem …

What happened were a succession of small indignities and humiliations piled on top of each other. When he displayed the slightest weakness or stumbled over his speech, the vicar would be on to it 'like a wild dog'.

> Even as I'm talking to you now I feel that if he was listening to this he'd be saying he's a wimp, he's a terrible wimp. I do feel very pathetic, babyish, yes childish, in his presence. The more he bullies me the more I feel it and the more I feel it the more he bullies me. So it's a vicious circle.

For some men, the feelings of emotional vulnerability and subordination contradicted an ideology of public masculinity, which created additional stress, as a male teacher discussed.

> I have come away and gone into my storeroom and sobbed, which again doesn't do a bloke's morale much good. Even though it is supposed to be a good human trait … You should be able to cope and I wasn't coping and I feel guilty that I wasn't coping. I'm a grown man and I should have been able to cope.

5.37 A woman teacher explained how her confidence and competence were systematically undermined, her class group was removed from her and when she used a spare desk in another teacher's classroom that was removed too. The behaviour of the head in picking on one person after another was acknowledged by many staff but they would not act collectively:

> He never bullied more than one person at one time. There were two groups: there were the people who had been through the mill, who

59

had suffered at his hands and there were the ones that he would make into a clique that were on his side ... One person would leave ... and then the whole staff would watch to see who was the next in line and keep their heads down and hope it wasn't them.

This particular teacher found that her inability to counter the head's behaviour led her to seek revenge in petty ways. She rang him up in the middle of the night and let down the tyres of his car. She spent thirteen weeks crying every day. She felt murderously violent towards him. 'I wanted to hit him. In the end I wanted to kill him. If someone had given me a gun I would have shot him.' She made vain attempts to start afresh in the school: 'I even went to him in the end and said, "I'll do anything you like, just tell me what I have to do to stop you treating me like this. Please can we start again." ' Rebuffed, she resigned her teaching post.

5.38   Another teacher had come into teaching late but worked successfully under two headteachers and was promoted twice within the school. However, a new headteacher took a dislike to him and a number of other staff.

> My life fell apart ... You'd be having an ordinary, calm discussion and you would say something which even afterwards you couldn't see why it caused a problem and there would be a sudden, almighty flare up, screaming and dancing, waving of arms, which I found totally intimidating. My stomach would churn. He'd got me into a total state of well, I can only say, scared that there was going to be another uproar. In the last few weeks before I left the school, it happened to me two or three times a week and occurred on a nearly daily basis with somebody else ... Kids notice atmosphere. Towards the end of the two years that all this took place, they used to commiserate with you. One boy would come in and say, 'The headmaster wishes to see you.' One boy, out loud, said, 'Oh dear, here you go again, what have you done this time?' which from a thirteen-year-old is terribly deflating for the teacher concerned ...

Thinking about it in retrospect he wished he had been able to make a resolute stand:

> Looking back it's so obvious that if I had responded to the first scream and dance ... with a very firm, 'No, I am not going to put up with this,' I might have stayed at least level if not on top. But I couldn't bring myself to do that. And under the screaming and shouting, I virtually cowered which I find very distressing ...

5.39   It is hard to convey, in these short extracts, how measured and convincing all these cases were. They were people who were overtaken by events, not needing or seeking conflict. However, they all described a neat story in which there was an identifiable bully carrying out identifiable unpleasantness towards a particular victim or group of victims. But abuses of power may be more pervasive and have a political dimension. They may surface through the isolated actions of a number of people acting to ensure that an institution operates in their interests. Of course, it is unreasonable to expect institutions to be always characterized by agreement about how they should be run. Conflict and struggle over ideals are an inevitable part of many people's working lives. But conflict turns to bullying when one person or side abuses their position of power to put down the people and ideas of those they see as opposed to them.

How much bullying goes on?

5.40   If we investigate bullying by trying to tease out its more subtle forms (the pervasive effects of bullying institutions on young people or adults, the occurrence of sexism or racism or classism or disablism and sexual or racial harassment) we may find that the incidence of bullying in our society is higher than indicated by the current figures for school bullying. While talking to a group of fifty teachers in Scotland about abuses of power in education, I asked them one of the same (rather strange) questions asked of children in the research: 'Who has been bullied sometimes or more often?' According to Mellor (1990), when this question was answered by students in relation to the previous term, 6 per cent of Scottish students, 6 per cent of Norwegian students and 22 per cent of students in a Sheffield study in England responded positively. About 70 per cent of my group of adults did so after we had raised each other's awareness of the issue.

ENDING CORPORAL PUNISHMENT IN SCHOOLS

5.41   Until recently corporal punishment was widely practised in schools in the UK as it still is in British homes. It is a practice devised by adults as a means of controlling other adults and children. Does its use by teachers and parents to children and young people go beyond the limits of the legitimate exercise of persuasion? Is it bullying, an abuse by teachers and parents of greater power and strength? Does its use contribute to the development of bullying between children and perhaps between adults? Or is its departure to be regretted as an essential feature of the relationship between adults and children, contributing positively to the upbringing and welfare of children?

5.42   I would argue that the ending of corporal punishment changed the basis of relationships between pupils and teachers and required a new view of punishment and control. It affected the conditions of learning in school and ideas about participation within the mainstream and exclusion from it. It can be seen as a significant step in the development of special education in the UK.

5.43   Until its abolition, corporal punishment was a popularly supported feature of school life. The Plowden Committee commissioned a survey in 1966 which showed that 90 per cent of teachers in England and Wales favoured its retention 'as a last resort' (Central Advisory Council for Education, 1967). I remember my dismay, when I went to work in

Nottingham in 1970, at the prevalence and acceptance of beatings. In London, where I worked previously, it was used but there was opposition to it. I did not encounter any teachers in Nottingham who dissented from its use, though there must have been some. As a newly qualified education psychologist, I wrote to a friend that I could hear the swishing of canes all over Nottingham from my office window.

5.44   Later, in Sheffield in the mid-seventies, I was called into a school by the headteacher of a large comprehensive school. He said he needed help with dealing with the problems he had with little girls: 'I know what to do with boys. I beat them. And I know what to do with big girls, because I beat them. But I don't know what to do with little girls because if I beat them I might hurt them.'

5.45   One of the places that corporal punishment occupied in the running of schools was as the last attempt to push young people into line before they were excluded, though its routine use in some schools belied the notion that it was held in reserve. Would abolition push up the number of exclusions or would a new 'last resort' emerge that would take on the significance of corporal punishment in the school culture? Or would the ending of corporal punishment reduce the culture of opposition between teachers and students?

5.46   Peter Newell has provided an account of abolition in *Children Are People Too: the case against physical punishment* (Newell, 1989), and I am indebted to him for several of the details of the story that follow. From 15 August 1987, in accordance with the 1986 Education Act, the use of corporal punishment was abolished in all state-funded schools in the United Kingdom and for any student on the assisted places scheme in private schools. The United Kingdom and the Republic of Ireland were the last of the European nations to permit the beating of school students. It was never allowed in Greece, was ended in the Netherlands in the 1820s and in Russia in 1917.

5.47   Flogging in the British Army was banned in 1906, birching as a judicial punishment was stopped in the United Kingdom in 1948, flogging in the Navy was ended in 1957, and corporal punishment for breaches of prison discipline was abolished in 1967. Was there something anachronistic and revealing of attitudes to children about retaining control through beating in schools when it was impermissible in prisons?

5.48   In 1951 the United Kingdom ratified the European Convention on Human Rights of which article 3 prohibited 'inhuman or degrading treatment or punishment'. It was this event, though not article 3, that was to create the pressure for a change in British practice. However, opposition to physical punishment was present from well before the advent of compulsory schooling in the nineteenth century. In 1669 a boy had presented a petition to Parliament protesting against 'that intolerable grievance our youth lie under, in the accustomed severities of the school discipline of this Nation' (quoted in Newell, 1989, p. 112). Stephen Humphries interviewed people born at the turn of the century who recalled how opposition to caning sometimes took the form of strikes, modelled on the strikes of parents and spread by reports in the press. As Joe Hopwood, who was a lamplighter born in Bristol in 1900, remembered:

> The teachers was hard in they days. They did cane you just for a little mistake in your work, you know. I've still got a mark on me finger where the teacher caned me. Well, there was a lot of fathers out on strike in Bristol in 1911. And on my way to school I saw on the content bill outside the newspaper shop: 'The London Schoolchildren on Strike For No Cane'. I ran down the lane into the playground an' started it. 'Come on, out on strike! Come on up the top an' see the bill.' And they all see'd it an' there was forty or fifty of us, and we all marched out of St Silas round the other schools to get the others out, singing an' shouting. We were going to get everyone out, then bide out 'til they says, 'No more cane.' But they locked em in by the time we arrived. It didn't work, so then we said, 'Come on, we'll go back.' That was the only time I remember playing truant, on that strike. We thought it might have done good, but it didn't. It done worse. They were just more determined. We got back 'bout twelve an' the headmaster lined us all up, 'Come on, hold 'em out!' an' we 'ad three of the best on the hand.
>
> (Humphries, 1981, pp. 97–98)

5.49   As with other educational issues, such as integration from the 1950s to the 1980s, practice lagged behind official rhetoric. The Newsom Report on 'early leavers' had shared 'the disquiet of those heads who feel that corporal punishment is likely to delay, rather than promote, the growth of self-discipline and that it is humiliating to staff and pupils' (Central Advisory Council for Education, 1963, p. 69). The Plowden Report on primary education adopted a clear line against corporal punishment arguing that 'the kind of relationship that ought to exist between teacher and child cannot be built up in an atmosphere in which the infliction of physical pain is regarded as a normal sanction' (Central Advisory Council for Education, 1967, p. 271). But progress towards abolition was resisted by the teaching profession and there was an equivocal stance from the unions. When Cardiff Education Authority attempted to introduce a ban in primary schools in 1968, opposition from local branches of teacher unions forced them to reintroduce it after two months.

5.50   In England, the initiative to start the campaigning organisation, STOPP (Society of Teachers Opposed to Physical Punishment) came from a London teacher, Gene Adams. When she started her teaching career in 1966 she was appalled by the personal vendetta waged by her headteacher against an eleven-year-old boy which included weekly canings (Newell, 1989, p. 113). Years of campaigning brought slow rewards. In 1973, the ILEA banned the cane from all its primary schools, and in 1979, the London Borough of Haringey became the first authority in the United Kingdom to introduce a ban in all its schools, though it could not enforce it in church schools.

The campaign in Scotland

5.51 The STOPP Campaign was concentrated in England. What was happening north of the border? In Scotland, before abolition, the use of a leather strap, or tawse, was a feature of most classrooms. Punishment was always on the hand rather than on the buttocks, which was common in England and Wales, and it did not acquire the same sexual connotations.

Activity 8 Memories of corporal punishment in Scotland

Cassette 2, Programme 3 is about the experiences of corporal punishment of a group of Scottish teachers when they were pupils themselves and later when they were teachers. It gives their view of the progress towards abolition, pushed forward by the actions of two mothers who took their opposition to corporal punishment to the European Court of Human Rights. Listen to the programme and then I will fill out some of the details in the story and ask about the implications of abolition for discipline and indiscipline in schools. The commentary is read by Marion Blythman who was at school in the 1940s in Glasgow, was later a teacher and headteacher, and subsequently head of the department of special needs at Moray House College of Education in Edinburgh.

5.52 In 1965 the Liaison Committee on Educational Matters, established by the Scottish Education Department, had set up a sub-committee on the 'elimination of corporal punishment in schools'. At its seventh meeting it agreed that 'the teaching profession should move towards ... gradual elimination'. It attempted to establish a code of practice for the use of the 'belt' by teachers which included the following:

- It should never be used for poor performance 'even if the failure appears to be due ... to inattention, carelessness or laziness'.

- It 'should not be used in infant classes'.

- 'In secondary departments, a girl should not be strapped by a man and as a general rule boys should not be strapped by women teachers'.

- It 'should not be inflicted for truancy or lateness unless the head teacher is satisfied that the child and not the parent is at fault'.

- It should be used as a last resort.

- It 'should be given by striking the palm of the child's hand with a strap and by no other means whatever'.

(adapted from SED, 1966)

5.53 These guidelines had only a limited effect in regularizing practice but at least became the starting point for discussions of belting among teachers in training. They had almost no impact on reducing the overall popularity of the belt.

5.54 The cases brought before the European Court of Human Rights concerned Gordon Campbell, aged 6, and Jeffrey Cosans, aged 15.

64

Mrs Campbell was refused an assurance that Gordon would not be belted in school and so kept him away from school, and Jeffrey's parents had supported their son in not accepting the belt for taking a short cut through a cemetery on his way home from school. Jeffrey was excluded from school until he would agree to abide by the school's disciplinary code. He never returned to school.

5.55   Their lawyer argued that the United Kingdom was in breach of two articles of the European Human Rights Convention. Article 3 states that 'No-one shall be subjected to torture or inhuman or degrading treatment or punishment'. Article 2 of protocol 1 to the Convention requires that in providing education, 'the State shall respect the rights of parents to ensure such education and teaching in conformity with their own religious and philosophical convictions'. The court ruled on 25 February 1982 that there had been a breach of Article 2 but not Article 3, partly because in the particular cases corporal punishment had not actually been administered.

5.56   When Lothian and Strathclyde took unilateral decisions to abolish the belt, they were greeted with tremendous opposition from EIS (the Education Institute of Scotland, the main teacher's union in Scotland):

> If a region adopted an early phasing out, it could not expect the co-operation of teachers. Teachers would hold themselves free to take action to protect themselves and their classes from violent or unruly pupils and the authority would have to accept responsibility for any exclusion from school and classroom.
>
> (*The Times Educational Supplement (for Scotland)*, 22 January 1982, p.1)

The union argued that teachers retained a common law right to use the belt and could be defended against dismissal provided they had previously informed the authority that they reserved this right (TESS, 22 January 1982, p. 5). However, unlike the DES, the Scottish Education Department urged compliance with the judgement of the European Court 'not to belt children whose parents they know are opposed to it'. The difficulty of maintaining such a two-tier system of those students who would and those who would not be subject to the belt prompted the Secretary of State for Scotland to write to the convention of Scottish Local Education Authorities to say that the belt should be banned from schools by 1983–4 'at the latest' (TESS, 1 July 1982, p. 1).

5.57   In the event, Lothian and Strathclyde implemented their ban with relatively little difficulty. The 'ladder of escalation' and the recording procedures recommended by the research project initiated by the Convention of Scottish Local Authorities (Cumming *et al.*, 1981), did produce an escalation of paperwork in many schools which was resented by teachers. I have included as Figure 2 the punishment algorithm issued to teachers at Ross High School in the Lothian Region. But this, like all top-down policies, was modified by many of the people who had to work with it. As one teacher remarked: 'It's a lot more work for the class teacher and for the head of department, so sensible teachers simply don't use it, particularly those who like their heads of department' (TESS, 20 August 1982).

Discipline Chain for the Classroom Teacher

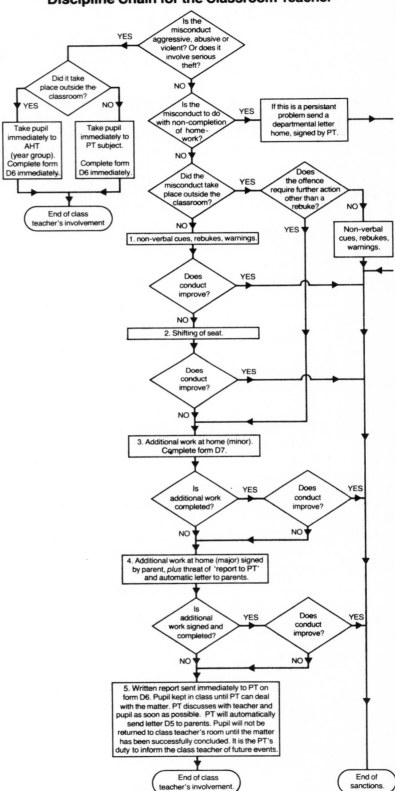

Figure 2 The punishment algorithm issued to Ross High School teachers (from The Times Educational Supplement, *20 August 1982, p. 4).*

English resistance

5.58   However, there was a backlash from the Conservative government in England where the 'junior minister responsible for schools, Dr Rhodes Boyson, ... made it clear he regards corporal punishment as an essential sanction for keeping order' (TESS, 1 July 1982, p. 1). In contrast to their counterparts north of the border, some of the southern teacher unions now supported the impetus for abolition. The 1982 conference of the NUT passed a resolution supporting the ban, and the following year the NUT was joined by the National Association of Head Teachers, the Secondary Heads Association, the Ulster Teacher's Union and the National Association of Welsh Teachers.

5.59   Because of the European judgement, the British government felt they had to do something but tried to do as little as possible. When Manchester Council tried to implement an authority-wide ban, 'the Crown' brought a prosecution, prompted by a local primary headteacher, and the court ruled that the ban was unlawful. However, in 1985, the government introduced a bill that would have permitted parents to exempt their children from corporal punishment in state schools. It passed through a first reading in the Commons but was seen as unworkable in the House of Lords which amended it and turned it into an abolitionist measure. The government withdrew the bill and when a new education bill was introduced the following year it contained nothing on corporal punishment. At committee stage in the Lords an abolitionist amendment was introduced. The government decided to allow a free vote on this amendment in the Commons with the Secretary of State for Education, Sir Kenneth Baker, urging a vote for retention. In the event abolition was passed by one vote, helped in farcical circumstances by Nancy Reagan and the wedding of Prince Andrew and Sarah Ferguson:

> The Prime Minister's absence at an official dinner for Mrs Nancy Reagan and the problems of a dozen MPs with pre-wedding traffic in Parliament Square may well have been decisive in giving the abolitionists a majority of a single vote. But one vote is enough. As a result from mid-August 1987, teachers who beat, tawse, cane or slap a state-supported pupil in any part of the United Kingdom will be open to civil proceedings for battery.
>
> (*The Times Educational Supplement*, 25 July 1986)

5.60   In fact, teachers using corporal punishment in state schools are liable to criminal or civil proceedings depending on the nature and degree of harm and decisions made by the young person involved, parents and the police. Battery or assault occasioning bodily harm are criminal offences. Civil proceedings, brought through a solicitor rather than the police and Crown, can be for emotional or physical damages and/or to take out an injunction to restrain a teacher from further similar actions.

5.61   The change in law permitted the use of force to avert violence or danger between students or in self-defence and it left the two-tier system

A redundancy of caning jokes: the market bottoms out in the 1980s.

Here endeth The Year of the Child

"There goes the last of the New Year resolutions."

Sorry Wilson. "Ne'er cast a clout 'til May is out", is nothing to do with the European Court of Human Rights

Well headmaster – after I'd caught him setting fire to the stock room and bearing in mind he'd recently inscribed 'up the hammers' on my new Metro I determined to set up an urgent meeting with his pastorial head, form tutor and probation officer with a view to calling in the educational psychologist – then I though 'what the hell' and clipped him round the earhole instead . . .

to operate in private schools ... a dubious privilege. When I was writing this, parents who sent their children to independent schools were still free to choose a school that would beat their children, though they may not be able legally to beat them themselves for much longer. The Scottish Law Commission has recommended that parents should be prevented by law from using any implement or any punishment which inflicts injury or prolonged pain in the course of discipline. Gradually, perhaps, the integrity of children's bodies will be accorded the same protection under law as that accorded to adults.

SUMMARY AND CONCLUSION

5.62   In this section I have discussed bullying in schools and in the workplace, sexual and racial harassment and sexist abuse, the development of anti-sexist strategies and the abolition of corporal punishment. I have included all these issues within an examination of abuses of power.

5.63   I considered the extent of bullying in schools and the subtle forms of school bullying which can take place beneath the unwitting gaze of teachers and parents. I argued that the extent and effect of bullying that takes place outside schools between siblings or between parents and children should not be minimized. It may often be the root of the bullying that surfaces in school. Though less frequently discussed, bullying is commonplace between adults at home or in the workplace where economic dependency carries particular risks and temptations to abuse power.

5.64   I considered the values of separating racial and sexual harassment from bullying more generally but could not see how bullying could be defined to exclude it. I looked at one detailed example of attempts to examine and reduce sexism in a primary school and hoped this might serve as an illustration of, and prompt to the development of ideas for improving other aspects of relationships in schools.

5.65   The section raised many issues but provided relatively few suggestions for reducing bullying in all its forms or for the development of appropriate strategies for discipline. I have concentrated instead on the groundwork; on the development of an understanding of bullying and the basis for discipline in the rights of the individual. The right to learn or work free from the threat of physical or psychological harm should be accorded to all of us, students (of any age), teachers and other school or college workers. An effective strategy to improve relationships in a school or workplace has to be based on a clear recognition of what can go wrong with those relationships. An approach within a school to combat sexism, sexual and racial harassment or bullying in general needs to apply to all members of the school community and to recognize the potential for abusing power in all of us.

6 STEMMING THE TIDE: PROVIDING SUPPORT?

6.1   In this final section of the unit I will look at some attempts to reduce the categorization of students as difficult or challenging in their behaviour and to reduce the difficulties students and teachers encounter. I will consider an attempt within a local authority to switch resources from segregated provision to mainstream support. I will provide examples from another authority of the range of activities in which behaviour support teachers are involved. I will ask whether attempts to curtail the power of local education authorities undermines the possibility of effective policies for reducing disaffection, disruption and exclusions and consider, briefly, an initiative in the Lothian Region of Scotland. This section prefaces the discussion of changing power relationships in education examined in detail in Units 14 and 15.

LOCAL AUTHORITY SUPPORT SERVICES

6.2   Some local authorities, then, have attempted to reduce the pressure to categorize students as having emotional and behaviour difficulties and send them to special schools by creating support services specifically for 'difficulties in behaviour'. Sometimes these operate alongside separate special provision and may even become, despite the apparent intention behind them, a way of channelling students into special schools or special units. This was what happened in Sheffield in the early 1980s, as documented by Carol Goodwin (1983). In the London Borough of Newham, they adopted a different approach by developing a behaviour support team to replace previously segregated secondary provision. The development of this provision was part of the Newham policy described in Unit 15 in which there was a clear commitment to phase out all special schools in the borough by 1996.

Activity 9   Challenging behaviour support

Now read 'Challenging behaviour support' by Paul Howard which is Chapter 33 in Reader 2. As you read it consider the following:

- the reasons for the change in policy;

- the difficulties of grafting a new policy onto old practices;

- the effects on schools of providing a support service that separates 'special educational needs (emotional and behavioural difficulties)' from other difficulties in learning.

6.3   The development of the Newham policy for 'behaviour support' grew out of a mix of planning and circumstance similar to that of the Grove School described in Unit 1/2. A secondary special school was running down, with rapid turnover of inexperienced staff. The solution to this problem had to fit with the Newham policy on integration described in Unit 15:

> Desegregating special education and thus meeting the needs of statemented children in mainstream schools will also contribute, by the entry of expert qualified staff into mainstream schools, to improve provision for the considerable number of children who already experience difficulties.
>
> (Newham Special Education Policy Statement, 1987; see Reader 2, Chapter 32, p. 381)

6.4   When the support service was set up, it became part of a fragmented secondary provision which also included a secondary support centre and a home tuition service, initially located in different parts of the borough. It also inherited those students at the special school for whom a mainstream place could not be found.

6.5   The initial expectation that resources and efforts would be concentrated on two secondary schools had to be changed when the schools concerned rejected this role. The service was also set up with the aspiration that schools would be persuaded to stop attributing classroom disruption to the emotional and behavioural difficulties of individual pupils and instead see them as arising out of a breakdown in relationships between teachers, students and curricula. They were to see the reduction of difficulties in behaviour primarily as their responsibility. They were to do this through a support service set up to deal specifically with difficulties in behaviour and retaining the label of the special school: 'special educational needs (emotional and behavioural difficulties)'. It would not be surprising if the support service had difficulties in explaining to schools that they were concerned with the processes of learning in schools for all students and not just those who had statements bearing the 'emotional and behavioural difficulties' label. The service ran in parallel with a support service for 'learning difficulties' and this might be seen as providing another barrier to a new view of behaviour difficulties for teachers in schools as well as support staff themselves. Paul Howard noted that the closure of the special school was followed by a 'slight increase' in out-of-borough referrals and this would need to be carefully monitored in checking the effects of the policy change. However, there had not been a clear rising trend in temporary or permanent exclusions which remained 'as unpredictable as in the past' (p. 390).

Supporting students, teachers and schools

6.6   In practice, the support service adopted a range of methods including 'support contracts', running support groups for teachers and providing in-service training sessions on difficulties in behaviour. In reading about the variety of approaches we may gain the impression that it is the schools who want individual solutions and the support teachers who want to change systems. However, support teachers themselves have a range of views. Some argue that all teachers must prove themselves first in work with students and only then can they expect schools to grant them the credibility for making suggestions about organizational and curriculum change. This view is parallelled by the rationale for the roles of learning support teachers in Scotland where effective 'consultancy' is seen to depend on the perception of a teacher's competence in co-operative teaching. Other support teachers sometimes take a further step, arguing that it is not their role to change students or to provide advice to schools but to work with either so that they develop a rationale and motivation to change themselves. This approach has its roots in theories and techniques of counselling.

Activity 10   Themes and variations in behaviour support work

In order to explore the range of activities of behaviour support workers, I asked one of our tutors, Bob Sproson, who is head of a 'behaviour support service', to write about the controversies which arise in the service in which he works and to provide cameos of his activities. I have included his contribution as Appendix 2 to this unit. As you read his article I suggest that you consider the following:

- How do the dilemmas aired by Bob Sproson compare with the issues raised by Paul Howard?

- Does eclecticism, drawing freely on a variety of approaches, involve a lack of clear principles and is this to be regretted?

- What do you see as the merits of the 'staff only' support role to which Bob Sproson alludes in the article?

- How does the exclusion of students affect the work of the support service?

- What range of approaches is illustrated by the examples of intervention?

6.7   Bob Sproson provides a vivid picture of a behaviour support service coming to terms with the changing power relationships in education in England and Wales. Set up by local education authorities, the services have suffered from the decreasing status of their sponsors. It has always been difficult for those working outside schools to attempt to influence what goes on inside them. But the devolution of funds to schools and the onus this places on support services to sell themselves (including their souls?) is pushing them to greater pragmatism and, perhaps, less 'eclecticism'. This is revealed particularly by the exclusion of students. If schools have been operating exclusions procedures cynically under the influence of a free market philosophy, should support teachers tell them so? And if they do, will they be able to retain their jobs? Now, many would argue that the *teachers* in behaviour support services or learning support services, and not just the money to pay for them, should be devolved to individual schools or groups of schools, as is the practice in some LEAs in England and Wales and is general practice in Scotland. The criticism of professionals external to the school rehearsed in Unit 1/2 has been that they lack detailed knowledge of the school and lack the power derived from status within the school to persuade others to implement their suggestions. One of the advantages of outsiders is that they offer an independent voice. But if schools become both the customers and, effectively, the employers of support services, is any scope left for professional independence?

6.8   The dilemmas raised in education by the 1988 Education Act are far more apparent in Bob Sproson's than Paul Howard's account. This is likely to be largely a result of the different policies and political complexions of their LEAs. Newham LEA has attempted to retain overall control and direction of educational policy. Cambridgeshire LEA pioneered devolution of management to schools and has been an enthusiastic supporter of government policies.

6.9   Bob Sproson argues that 'virtually any considered educational approach must have some merit' as a justification for his 'eclecticism'. In practice, his eclecticism has narrower limits than this. Would he approve of punitive approaches involving severe withdrawal of privileges such as the one which culminated in the 'pin down' regime used in Staffordshire and described in Unit 1/2 (pp. 27–8)? Probably the orginators of this regime would have regarded it as both 'considered' and 'educational'. Further, the 'counselling of teachers' role adopted by some of his colleagues is not one that he finds attractive: 'Anyone would be foolish to go in [to a school] under the label of "expert" suggesting that they have all the solutions. It is a recipe for disaster to go in with none!'

6.10   To what extent are behaviour support teachers forced to take on teachers' views of students? Bob Sproson argues that problems in schools can be generated and exacerbated by insensitive teachers. Yet he sees the first step in working with students to be a clear statement of 'the nature and frequency of the "problem" behaviour'. This would appear to involve the acceptance of the teachers' definition of the situation. I would replace this initial step with 'a clear analysis of the nature of the difficulty' which involved the perspectives of all those involved. However, Bob Sproson does say that 'the aim is not to mould that pupil in accordance with the beliefs and philosophies of the practitioner'. Is there an ambiguity and ambivalence here?

6.11   Compulsory school uniforms are a perennial focus of dispute in schools and are frequently an element in the exclusion of students in England and Wales (uniforms cannot be compulsory in Scotland). I would find it very difficult to support schools in attempts to enforce the wearing of school uniform. I see the choice of clothing as a right of students, as an important aspect of their developing autonomy and the insistence on a compulsory uniform as an abuse of power. However, I could work with students as a friend and advocate and this would include helping the student to 'survive today'. Would the limits to my pragmatism exclude me from working as a support teacher?

6.12   About twenty students spend some time at the behaviour support base. A colleague of Bob Sproson's suggested that many of them were excluded for swearing and said she wondered 'where these teachers are half the time' though she acknowledged that 'it's the venom behind the words that they [i.e. the teachers] can't take'.

6.13   She had approached the job from a counselling background and counselling had been emphasized by the previous head of the centre. While she had a preference for working with staff to enhance their capacities for coping with difficulties with students 'since it was the teachers who had day-to-day responsibilities', she found that she was working increasingly with students. To illustrate the range of her work she mentioned the support she was giving to one teacher who had become the confidante of a student who had been sexually abused and a student she was seeing regularly who had been bullying other students. She felt that the students she saw 'all have in common very low self-esteem'. Once schools accepted her role in counselling students, there could be an unrealistic demand on her time. She complained that at one school, 'All I can give them is 20 minute slots with the occasional 40 minutes … Usually I've been told by various members of staff: "For god's sake do something about so-and-so's behaviour." I'm confused, I don't feel I'm doing a clean job. It's not counselling because they don't come to me voluntarily.' She agreed with Bob Sproson that the pressures produced by imminent exclusions were affecting the nature of their work and their capacity for improving the lives of students and their teachers.

6.14   Schools which refuse to take students excluded from other schools, who are not the subject of a statement specifying a special school, are in breach of the law. Yet, while this may be the case in law, there appears to be very little that LEAs in England and Wales are able to do in practice following local management of schools, and this applies equally to schools rejecting students who are recommended for a mainstream place after attending a special school. David Sassoon (1992) assistant director for schools in the London Borough of Brent, argues that the effective diminution in power occurs because the LEAs are no longer the employers of teachers under local management of schools:

> Should the headteacher of a school refuse to admit she or he can be overruled by the Chief Education Officer (CEO) of the LEA. If opposition persists, the CEO could discipline the headteacher, if necessary by suspending her or him (i.e. in a school that does not have control of its formula-funded budget) and referring the matter to a disciplinary committee of the Council …
>
> In the school that has control of its formula-funded budget the CEO has profound difficulties in making her or his instruction stick, especially if the recalcitrant headteacher has the support of the governors.
>
> (Sassoon, 1992, p. 56)

6.15   In all three examples which Bob Sproson chose to illustrate his work, the exclusion of the student from school was a central feature. This reflects the dramatic effects that exclusion is having on the work of behaviour support services and the pressing national need to understand the effect of the 1988 Education Act on exclusions and to do something about it. Neither the Department of Education and Science (now the Department for Education) nor the Scottish Office Education Department publish statistics on exclusions, although the Department of Education and Science started to look at permanent exclusions in 1991 (see para. 3.26). One of Bob Sproson's examples concerned a child in care, and it is an interesting irony of legislation that children in care cannot be the subjects of education supervision orders, despite the fact that many of them may not attend school regularly.

LOTHIAN'S YOUTH STRATEGY

6.16   Depending on your point of view, Scotland has so far escaped from, or has not been privileged to participate in, the full changes to the education service written in to the 1988 Education Act. In 1992, local management of schools has not been implemented in Scotland and many schools do not have boards of governors. The relationship between schools and regional authorities remains far closer than in England and Wales. No schools have opted out of local government control. Authorities in Scotland have retained the power to introduce authority-wide policies with the expectation that they will be adopted in all schools.

6.17   Lothian Region decided to reduce difficulties in behaviour in schools by introducing a co-ordinated strategy which mobilized resources in education and social services. The youth strategy, begun in 1985, was to conform to principles 'concerned with keeping children and young people at risk of being excluded [from school], or having to leave home or with special educational needs, as far as possible, with their own families, neighbourhoods and local schools' (Lothian Regional Council, 1992, para. 1.2).

6.18   Initially the strategy was funded and developed for students of secondary age, though it was extended to primary schools in 1990. All secondary schools have a school liaison group, chaired by the head or a representative of the head and involving teachers, an education welfare officer, an educational psychologist and a social worker. Parents may be invited to participate in the work of the group but their attendance is not automatic ('school liaison groups should consider the possibility of inviting parents to participate in the discussion') (Lothian Regional Council, 1992, para. 2.8). The involvement of students in discussion is not stressed.

6.19   The strategy co-ordinates work of a variety of agencies involved with students and schools are expected to link difficulties in behaviour and learning. At Drummond Community High School, for example, there is a curriculum support team which provides 'the main thrust of youth strategy provision in the school along with learning support and English as a second language teachers'. The school has summarized its youth strategy in the following way:

- A commitment to providing all our pupils with an appropriate education and only in exceptional circumstances seeking full time alternatives outwith the school or permanent exclusion.

- Recognition of the crucial importance of the quality of the curriculum experience offered to pupils and the need to evaluate this experience and provide support for development and improvement.

- The need for all pupils to have an adequate support structure offered through Guidance [pastoral staff], Learning support/English as second language staff, curriculum support and external agencies and *for this support to be properly co-ordinated.*

- The need for teachers to have support in dealing with classroom management and curriculum development, not only through in-service and staff development, but also through direct, interactive support in the classroom.

(Drummond Community High School, 1990, p. 1)

6.20   Lothian Region has been keeping a careful watch on exclusions from school. Since the introduction of the youth strategy and in contrast to all the indications from England, the numbers of informal exclusions and formal exclusions (lasting 5 days or more) have dropped in secondary schools. Between school years 1989–90 and 1990–91 there was a 28 per cent drop in formal exclusions and a 5 per cent drop in informal exclusions. However, in primary schools there was an opposite trend; for the same time period formal exclusions had increased by 64 per cent and informal exclusions had increased by 32 per cent. Those with responsibility for the youth strategy argue that if comparable additional resource were provided for the primary sector it would show 'comparable results' (Lothian Regional Council, 1991, p. 9).

CONTROL FROM THE CENTRE OR SUBSIDIARITY?

6.21   The notion of subsidiarity, that decisions should be made as close as possible to those who are affected by them, has become increasingly aired in the early 1990s, as a concept with which to combat the pressure to increase the power of central organizations in the European Community and decrease the jurisdiction of member states over their own affairs. One of the problems with the concept is that it can be used to justify quite different practices. Is the Cambridgeshire example of central services hoping to be bought in by devolved locally-managed budgets a better example of grassroots involvement than the youth strategy in Lothian where the region retains control to direct *and* fund at the school level, policies on disruption, integration and truancy? In Units 14 and 15 you will have an opportunity to consider in detail some of the government policy changes and pressures that have surfaced in the discussion of practices in this section.

SUMMARY AND CONCLUSION

6.22   In this section, I have described some attempts to reduce exclusions from schools and segregated placements resulting from perceived difficulties with student behaviour. The behaviour support services in the London Borough of Newham and in Cambridgeshire felt that involvement was most effective before dramatic confrontations arose Yet in both areas it was found to be extremely difficult to change the culture of schools who wished to pass on responsibility for difficult behaviour to others, particularly at points of crisis.

6.23   This section did not give the detail of attempts by particular schools to reduce devaluation and disaffection. You will have to consider how such efforts, coupled with work to create appropriate curricula for all students, might reduce difficulties in behaviour and obviate the need for external support.

6.24   Teachers and other professionals who attempt to change the relationships or curricula in schools from the outside may have insufficient awareness of priorities within a school, insufficient knowledge of the way to effect change in that institution or may simply lack the power to make a difference. Bob Sproson provided a graphic illustration of these difficulties in a support service where the power of the backing from the Local Education Authority had been curtailed. In Scotland the regional authorities have retained greater powers, and in Lothian they used this to promote their 'youth strategy' within secondary schools based on enhanced staffing within the schools and regional authority co-ordination.

7   INVESTIGATIONS

7.1   There are many possible investigations which fall within the title 'Happy Memories'. You could investigate adults' experiences of disaffection, discipline, bullying in education or of truancy from school. You could visit and evaluate specialist provision or learn about the working lives of education welfare officers, behaviour support teachers, or pastoral care/guidance staff in secondary schools. You might delve into the meaning for people of the phrase 'a proper regard for authority'. You might investigate disciplinary strategies of parents and compare these with disciplinary approaches of teachers. You might survey attitudes to corporal punishment in the home. You could look at the significance of uniform and the part it plays in the control of and conflicts with students. You could survey practices in the schools in your area and ask teachers and students whether and why it should be worn and about appropriate sanctions for failures to conform. I have set out four of these possibilities in a little more detail below.

Memories of conflict

7.2   Interview a group of four adults of varying ages about their memories of school discipline and breaches of discipline and how they were affected by it. What are their current views about the way school discipline should be maintained and how has it been affected by their own experiences?

7.3   I suggest that you think out, carefully, the questions you wish to cover. Try to get at their understanding of 'authority' inside and outside schools.

Understanding special provision

7.4   Try to arrange to spend a day or half-day at a special school or unit for students categorized as having emotional and behavioural difficulties. Spend some of the time talking with the students about their past and present experiences of education. How do they see their move to the school or unit? How does the curriculum they engage in compare with work in their previous school? How do the views of staff about the nature and purpose of the provision compare with that of students?

What does an education welfare officer do?

7.5   Obtain the documents from your local authority concerned with the policies and job descriptions for education welfare officers and arrange to interview one or two education welfare officers about the detail of their day-to-day activities. How do these activities fit in with the policy documents? Try to work out with your informant(s) what they would see as their ideal job description. Consider and analyse the constraints placed on their work.

Bullying amongst adults

7.5   Using the ideas within this unit, analyse your experience as an adult of direct and institutional bullying or harassment. Choose adults whom you think have different background and experience from yourself and compare their knowledge and experience of bullying with your own. Construct a bullying scenario, depicting a setting and an event seen from the perspectives of a 'victim', a 'bully' and an 'onlooker'. Compare reactions and resolutions to it provided by your informants.

78

APPENDIX 1 CONVERSATION BETWEEN FELICITY ARMSTRONG AND NIGEL H

NIGEL I never used to go to school every day ... because some of the lessons didn't really interest me and some of the teachers I didn't really get on with. Those were my primary reasons for not going really. The lessons I used to enjoy, yes, these were worth going to. I'd go there, partake in the lesson, be an active part of it. But certain lessons and certain teachers – it wasn't worth the hassle going there. You'd sit back and think: Is it worth the hassle? And so much pressure put on you, sort of thing. You think: no, maybe I won't. Like – I didn't do my homework, wouldn't go – reasons like that. I didn't really dislike school – I enjoyed most of it, but like I said, at St A's I took rakes and rakes and rakes of time off.

There were only a couple of teachers that picked on us – one was the maths teacher – she used to pick on us. There were five of us, all friends and we all got split up in the lesson and after that it just got worse. She'd still pick on us. Some of us would just take days off when that lesson was coming up. We'd say, 'Oh, I'm not going, I'll see you at so and so,' and meet up a bit later, and it was good fun. But as I say, I didn't really dislike school. I didn't stay away because of problems at home or anything like that. If there's a problem at home you don't go home. If there's a problem at school you don't go to school; do you know what I mean? It's like anything in life I suppose. If there's a problem at work, you don't go to work – you make some excuse.

My mum knew I was playing truant. She wasn't able to do anything really. I'd set off for school and by the time I got there, I'd be late; then I'd think, 'Oh, it's not worth the hassle going in because I'm late.' I used to go somewhere on the way to school and I'd think, 'No, I'll go to Summertown instead,' and at maybe 12 o'clock I'd go home for dinner and say, 'There's no lessons in the afternoon' (not to arouse my mum's suspicions too much). And she'd think, 'They have an awful lot of days off at that school.' But she never got to the stage of thinking, 'There's a truancy problem somewhere' – so she was quite all right about it really.

Yes, this was after my dad died. If he'd been alive I don't think I'd have done it so much. I definitely don't think I'd have done it.

I kept certain people at school fairly sweet so they wouldn't send a letter home. I kept in with the headteacher and most of them quite well. They said, 'Make sure you come in,' or 'Buck up your ideas or else.'

I wasn't so much a trouble maker in school but I'd be there if there was trouble. I wouldn't call myself a trouble maker.

FELICITY I can remember when you were at primary school and you used to love school. You used to walk up the street with me and tell me everything you'd been doing that day.

NIGEL Yes, I used to love school. I'll tell you – teachers, if you treat them right, they're like ordinary people. You can have a great laugh with them.

When I went to college I used to get on with the lecturers fantastically; I still go back and visit some of them. But it doesn't mean I never had no problem with any teachers. But it was just the odd ones who thought I was a bit too cocky for my own good.

Our group was picked on by some teachers. We were quite disruptive; we used to disrupt the class basically. We weren't picked on from a racist point of view. There were quite a few other black kids there, in fact, loads of black and Asian kids and mainly we were quite smart and intelligent. We just had a bit too much lip for our own good so the teacher thought, 'I don't need this,' which I can't blame them. But we didn't do it in all the classes. Classes that really did interest us, we'd think, 'Yeah, fantastic!' But take the maths class. Some of the maths interested us or we'd think, 'We've done this before so we think there's no point.' And then we hit this communication thing when we wanted to do certain exams. The teacher said, 'Oh, well, no. I don't think you've got the ability to do it.' And from there on we thought, 'Oh well, if you're not going to give us the chance ... '

I wasn't too happy at all about it. I had to pay to go in for the exam myself; there were quite a few of us who did that. But after I'd paid for it, I thought, 'My God, you haven't entered me. I've had to pay to be entered myself.' And by the time it came to the actual exam, I thought, 'I'm not doing it now – you couldn't be bothered to enter me and I wasted my money and didn't go to the exam.'

Yes, it affected my confidence badly. Actually, I was really pissed off about it. I thought, 'You've got no confidence in me. Me and you don't get on.' Me and the rest of the lads, we thought if we put our minds to it, we had the ability to do it. I think one out of the five of us got entered.

FELICITY I remember when I was teaching English and I wanted to enter some people for the old O Level exam, the head of department would say, 'Don't enter her. She couldn't do it and it's not fair to encourage her.' Often pupils couldn't afford to pay for themselves anyway. They'd sometimes take the O Levels they weren't allowed to take at school a year later at the CFE. By that time they'd lost a year and lost their self-confidence.

NIGEL At school we were told, 'If you get this and you get that, you'll get a job.' Well I got 'this' and I got 'that' and I didn't get a job. So I thought, 'Hmm. That's not very wise, is it.' I don't think they conditioned anybody for the outside world, which is a totally different ball game as far as I'm concerned.

I went into plumbing out of desperation actually to get a decent job. I left school and I wanted to be an electrician. I took a special test for it called the CITB test and they said, 'If you get an A you've definitely got a job.' Well, I went to take this test and I got an A grade and I went to about 30 employers and had interviews and I didn't get a job, so in the end I just had to settle for what I could get. There were jobs available. I haven't a clue why I didn't get one. Well – I don't know. Maybe at the time – you don't see many black construction workers – at the time, maybe, they thought, 'You're not suitable for the job mate.' I just thought, 'I can't believe this.' I've got an A grade and there are guys with B grades getting the jobs I was going for and I was thinking, 'Hold on. I've got an A grade.'

APPENDIX 2   THEMES AND VARIATIONS IN BEHAVIOUR SUPPORT

Bob Sproson

The ongoing dilemma of behaviour support work is whether the task is to provide 'alternative education' for those pupils who are deemed too difficult for mainstream school or if it is to provide 'in-school support' for pupils; this is further complicated by the fact that there is much disagreement as to the best way to approach both aspects of the work. Alternative provision can be viewed as being made at a centre by a small number of staff, or as part of a whole range of resources which schools can access as extensions to their curricula. In-school support work can be interpreted in a variety of ways, but simplistically divides into work with staff and work with pupils.

VARIETIES OF SUPPORT

I am a confirmed eclectic. It seems to me that virtually any considered educational approach must have some merit. I would, however, reject two absolute extremes of the spectrum of thinking.

The first is a notion of staff support wherein the supporter not only rejects any suggestion on the part of the school that he/she will do any direct work with pupils, but also does not see his/her role as being to offer strategies or advice to the teacher: the role is one of enabling or empowering the teacher to clarify his/her own ideas. The suggestion is that there will be a two-fold benefit for the teacher: first, he/she will feel better about him/herself personally and professionally because he/she has been given individual support time; and secondly, in that time, the support teacher will have acted as a 'sounding board' for that teacher and enabled him/her to develop clear plans as to how to work with the 'difficult' pupil. I would not deny that this process can be worthwhile, but the support teacher should have practical advice available and ideally a sound base of teaching experience to call upon on which to base that advice. While anyone would be foolish to go in under the label of 'expert', suggesting that they have all the solutions, it is a recipe for disaster to go in with none!

At the other extreme the notion of a behaviour support teacher going along to a school and suggesting that they can take its problems away is doomed! In this service we work with 21 secondary schools; if we took away only the 'worst' pupil in each year from each school we would have 105 pupils to educate with neither the physical nor human resources to meet their needs – and they might just constitute a difficult group!

Having rejected these extremes, I suggest that the dilemma is unnecessary. A preventive in-school support model cannot remove the need for reactive 'crisis' work. The two must be provided together.

What then is the role of a behaviour support teacher? Ideally he/she should be able to offer a school as wide a range of skills as possible, from working with staff groups on whole-school policies, through suggesting strategies which teachers might employ, clarifying the nature of behavioural difficulties, offering in-class support, providing individual support to the pupil and possibly to the family/carers, teaching the class while the teacher is able to give individual time to the 'difficult' pupil, co-ordinating the work of other relevant agencies, to providing or keying into supplements/alternatives to the timetable.

My own experience leads me to believe that teachers have most respect, in this area of work, for fellow professionals who they believe would be capable of performing well in the classroom, and indeed, who are willing to 'roll up their sleeves' and provide practical help.

Having suggested an eclectic approach to the role of the support teacher, I would argue that when working with individual pupils a similarly wide view of strategies is required. I worry greatly when I hear practitioners say they adopt behaviourist, therapeutic or any other specific approaches. Different approaches work with different pupils, and may even be effective under different circumstances with the same pupil. The important aspects are that:

- the nature and frequency of the 'problem' behaviour is clearly stated;

- a plan/programme is formulated to combat the problem;

- the effectiveness of this is carefully monitored and alternative strategies employed if no success is achieved.

This may seem to be a behaviouristic approach, and I would accept that clear description and monitoring are central to any behaviour modification programme. But the plan or programme which is devised should draw upon as wide a range of techniques and approaches as possible. The starting point of any plan should be what that particular pupil needs to enable him/her to behave in a more 'appropriate' manner; the aim is not to mould that pupil in accordance with the beliefs and philosophies of the practitioner.

In an article in *The Times* (19 October 1991) on the role of the social worker under the new Children Act, a social worker stated that she had originally come into the work to 'change the world' but now accepted that she needs to work with individuals to support them in an unfair world. There is much here that translates to behaviour support work. Very often it is clear that a more flexible 'system' would better meet the needs of an individual and that 'problem behaviours' occur in particular situations in which pupils are compelled to remain. There is work to be done to get legislators to realize the need for flexibility, and to help educational institutions, and the individuals who work within them, to address their own 'behaviour', and to examine its effects upon the subsequent behaviour of their pupils. But any such work is likely to be 'long-term' – the pupil has to survive today, and will need 'support' to do that.

DEALING WITH DIFFICULT TEACHERS

When working in schools we often come up against two particular problems. First, it is often difficult to overcome the 'goodies for baddies' argument. When we offer positive alternatives for pupils, staff can find it difficult to move out of 'punishment mode' – why should a pupil get this when he/she is behaving badly? Secondly, the very small number of 'bad' teachers create enormous difficulties. By 'bad', I mean those teachers who create an environment within which certain pupils find it impossible to survive. This may either be due to the content of their teaching or, more usually, their attitude towards the pupils, or indeed, a mixture of both. Some pupils may find appropriate defence mechanisms which enable them to survive, others are forced into aggressive, inappropriate or unacceptable defences which lead to their rapid exclusion from the school. Almost inevitably, it is the teachers who create such problems, who are unwilling to address the possibility that their own teaching style or behaviour is contributing to their difficulties.

It is impossible to place such 'bad' teachers in a simple category; they may be young or old, experienced or inexperienced, junior or senior in the staff group, possibly working within a school which has an ethos with which they are unable to identify. Whoever they are, whatever the reason, their work can be very destructive. For the very vulnerable pupil, there only needs to be one badly handled, conflict situation which 'explodes' and all the hard work by the pupil, the school and the support services can be wasted.

Behaviour support staff working regularly with pupils may find that the names of one or two teachers crop up time and again when pupils discuss the difficulties they find in school. Even given the likelihood that pupils will present a partial or exaggerated view, there is a clear need to question these teachers' methods. But what do we do then? The only professional approach is to take the problem to the senior management of the school. When this happens, the members of the senior management team are usually aware of the problem but find it immensely difficult to address. I would not minimize the difficulties involved at all, but the responsibility must rest with them, although it is not, of course, inconceivable that the teacher involved is a member of that group. Perhaps appraisal will help schools to look at such issues.

83

The problems which we face in supporting 'troublesome' pupils can only be exacerbated by the 1988 Education Act and present government thinking, indeed by the increased pressure on all teachers. It is very difficult to convince teachers that they should persevere with the pupil who continually 'undermines' all that they do in a lesson and even pops his/her head in to disturb lessons he/she should not be in. The pressure on heads to market their schools, to publish results and attendance figures and to go through copious paperwork if they wish to 'except' pupils from part of the national curriculum, make the prospects seem bleak for pupils who are low achievers, poor attenders or who present behaviour problems. Equally, pressures on teachers to achieve good academic results with their classes, to get pupils through attainment levels, and the possibility of teachers' salaries being linked to such results make it increasingly unlikely that pupils who do not fit the system or prevent others from gaining maximum benefit will survive in the mainstream.

A leading article in *The Times Educational Supplement* (25 October 1991) effectively illustrates a further problem: it is far cheaper for schools to go through the exclusion process than to 'buy into' expensive support services. The article cites research carried out by Margaret Stirling at Westminster College, Oxford, in which she concludes that 'headteachers thought them [exclusions] better [i.e. cheaper] than other routes which keep a child in a school though they do eventually provide extra support.' Thus, although it is possible to gain access to additional support for 'difficult' pupils, either through 'buying in' available services or through pursuing a statement of special educational need, it is very difficult for heads to see the attraction of maintaining the pupil in the school when a straightforward exclusion will remove the problem. One deputy head had commented that 'exclusions are a way of getting rid of your problems and you don't have to fork out large sums of money as a result'. At present a head can list a pupil as on roll on 7 January, receive the AWPU (age weighted pupil unit) for that pupil and then exclude him/her on 8 January. I know of no head who would intentionally do this, but for a head who is under financial pressure and often pressure from certain staff to 'take effective action', or to 'make an example of' a pupil, the attractions of rapid exclusion over prolonged and costly support are all too obvious.

Growing exclusions increase pressure on a support service to make alternative provision and this inevitably has a detrimental effect upon 'preventive' support work; the balance swings towards 'crisis' management. In Cambridge, heads are being told that support services will provide them with what they want – the carrot to tempt them not to opt out is that the LEA will work in partnership with them to provide the services they require. The demand which they make upon this service may well be for alternative provision. Hopefully if that is the case, we can prevent the return to 'sin-bin' thinking, and develop a range of positive resources which schools will find attractive.

Who holds the responsibility for educating according to age, ability and aptitude or for providing access to the National Curriculum for those children who are excluded? At present it must be the LEA, but how does it fund the work if the finances have all been devolved to schools? Moreover, if all schools go for grant-maintained status, if LEAs cease to exist, where then does the responsibility lie?

I fear that present government thinking and legislation is unable to genuinely encompass the needs of these young people. In many cases this 'pressure effect' will be counter-balanced by the sheer determination and professionalism of teachers to meet the needs of all their pupils. But they and the pupils will need enormous support from the likes of ourselves in the support services, if the number of pupils segregated from mainstream provision because they present behavioural difficulties is not to continue to grow.

EXAMPLES OF INTERVENTION

I have cited here three case studies, chosen because they illustrate some pertinent issues. They are not chosen to show what 'good work' we do, but some of the difficulties we face. I think that many professionals find it very hard to say 'I don't know where we go from here' – but in at least one of these cases, I needed to say that. I believe, truly, that honesty helps! I have fictionalizd the students' names.

John

John first came to my notice when I was invited to a 'planning' meeting by the school support officer, the representative of the senior education officer with responsibility for that school. 'Planning' was a euphemism, as the school had already decided that exclusion was inevitable and as this was John's third secondary school (he had been excluded from the previous two) the LEA had decided that a further mainstream placement was inconceivable. Over to you, Bob! Any support service in its infancy will meet this difficulty and those which subscribe purely to making provision when mainstream placements have broken down will meet it continually. I felt that it was much too late to involve me when the school was about to exclude a pupil. But, interestingly, we did have a support teacher working in the school who was offering 'staff only' support. She was seen as ineffective by the school senior management, and therefore not consulted.

I duly attended the 'planning' meeting together with the member of my staff who has responsibility for Year 11 alternative provision (although John was still in his tenth year). At the meeting we accepted responsibility for John and subsequently set about putting together as good a programme as we could in the circumstances and co-ordinating our efforts with social services who were involved too. We claim £120.00 per term from the 'referring' school where no provision is made in school, but have no other funding to meet this need. The member of staff responsible for alternative provision charged with this responsibility has to weave some magic. He has no full-time staff, but I ask all members of the team to provide one session per week for the 'centre students'; this is not a part of the job description which is taken on by all with enthusiasm. Wherever possible, we use community resources such as FE colleges, work experience, the YMCA or the sports centre. We prefer this model to full-time attendance at the centre as it moves away from the sin bin/dumping syndrome.

Initially John attended very little that we set up for him. It transpired that he was spending very little time at home, but a great deal at a notorious local address. Case conferences followed at which the remaining residential establishments funded by social services showed little desire to 'take John on'. In their view, 'he will not commit himself to work positively with us, therefore we cannot work with him'. John learned very quickly that if he said 'no' or metaphorically or literally 'stuck up two fingers', nothing happened. Eventually, after we made a great deal of fuss, John was admitted to a residential community home some twenty miles away while we awaited a vacancy at the local 'hostel' which also still serves as a remand home. Once at this establishment, he began to attend sessions in core studies and woodwork at the centre and to participate in soccer and canoeing sessions. Although we were never able to engage him in any work experience programmes – 'I ain't working for no bread, man!' – John did attend the remainder of his programme with some consistency and success. Without doubt he is a very able young man and very capable of planning his future. The values on which he bases those plans are, however, questionable; he intends to have a good time, make some money (illegally – though he would not be foolish enough to commit the offences himself – only live off the profits), and will only reconsider when he is convinced that he is not able to live a good life in this manner. The reality may be that he will not be forced to reconsider!

Once a bed became available at the hostel, John moved in – now back full-time in Cambridge, his attendance slowly worsened as he became more deeply involved with the local 'criminal' fraternity. In June of 1990 the centre was burgled (and has since been burgled with monotonous regularity – although no-one has been charged to date) and since then John has steadfastly refused to attend any sessions at all. He now lives between various addresses and the hostel (without bail conditions his movements cannot be restricted by hostel staff) and in five months has attended no educational placement.

What do we do? In accordance with the Children Act, we can either plump for prosecution for non-attendance or take out an education supervision order. Since John is officially 'in care', should the LEA prosecute the social services? [But see comment in para. 6.15.] Even if it was felt that there was anything positive in one local government department suing another, the LEA would be in a very difficult position as it is not making a school place available. The problem with an education supervision order is that there are no further resources available, so the taking out of an order would achieve nothing. In previous years John would have been an obvious candidate for the Community Home with Education system, but Cambridge has no such in-county provision now and at this stage in his school career an 'out-county placement' will not be considered. What next?

Keith

As head of the service, I think it inconceivable that I can do my job properly if I do not take on some of the 'in-school' work and the alternative provision. As an example of the former, I was asked to provide support to Keith, a ninth year pupil at a local village college. Again I became involved at far too late a stage, though this is inevitable with a new service. I met Keith on a Tuesday and was beginning to prepare an intervention programme when on Thursday he was excluded indefinitely. After meeting with the head and relevant staff, the prospects of Keith making a successful return to the school seemed minimal. I could not know whether the staff view of Keith's behaviour was a 'fair' one, but I could see that feeling among the staff was running at such a level that they would ensure, probably unconsciously, that any return was unsuccessful.

I have subsequently done a great deal of work in this college and hold it in very high regard. Given the relationship that we now have, I might now consider at least further discussions with staff at this stage, but then I was convinced that transfer was in everyone's best interest. My role developed as a mediator between the head and the parents, who were very committed and eloquent, between Keith and his parents, as an adviser to the parents, a seeker of possible school places, a 'preparer' with Keith for his introduction to a new school, and very importantly, a worker with the receiving school staff in developing strategies in working with Keith. This last part of the work was done together with the team member who held the responsibility for the work in that school. That transfer took place 15 months ago and the new placement has been successful – not just, I would argue, in that Keith has survived, but in that he is achieving academic success and social acceptance to a degree which had not previously appeared feasible.

Jason

Jason is an eighth year pupil at another Cambridgeshire village college. Again our involvement occurred at 'crisis' stage, again the support teacher allocated to the college previously had been singularly unsuccessful having pursued the 'staff only' model. I had begun to develop a good relationship with senior staff at the college and was meeting with them to plan for the allocation of a new behaviour support teacher. During these discussions problems with Jason escalated very quickly. He is a boy with a violent temper and, although he is small, he finds it very difficult to refrain from quite brutal attacks on other pupils. I will not dwell on his difficulties or the school's admirable attempts to support him. However, the case highlights two problems. There is a confusion within Cambridgeshire as to how exclusion procedures dovetail with special needs procedures. Secondly, there are difficulties for a support service which is about to become an 'agency' and therefore to be 'bought in' by schools, when the head of the school concerned does not think that the LEA policy for the service meets the schools' needs.

Cambridgeshire has a newly developed five phase policy for special needs. Briefly summarized this is:

1 Identification of need

2 School adapts curriculum content or delivery or allocates increased help to the pupil from its own resources

3 External agency involved

4 Educational psychologist involved

5 Formal assessment

No request for assessment is considered unless work at the previous stages has been carried out and is documented. In this instance Jason had reached stage 4, but the educational psychologist had not recommended formal assessment and Jason therefore returned to Phase 3. An attack on another pupil then led to Jason's exclusion and the head now pressed for special school placement. County policy states that formal assessment must take place in the host school and cannot take place whilst a pupil is excluded. The head was unwilling to re-admit Jason for the assessment to take place even though the educational psychologist now saw assessment as necessary and the LEA would not pursue assessment whilst Jason was excluded.

With regard to the second issue, the school support officer who had previously enjoyed an excellent relationship with the head, now found that relationship threatened and began to doubt the prospect of her services being 'bought in' in future. She was being asked, in effect, 'whose side are you on?' Under LMS, services will no longer be centrally funded and provided to schools; schools will be given an increased budget, decide how much provision they require from a service and buy that amount. If they do not like what they receive or what is on offer, the service will not be bought and will presumably cease to exist. Support services will have to convince schools of their worth and will find it very difficult to question practice, or adopt a critical stance.

Although these problems appeared insoluble for a time after 'discussions' (at great length!), compromises were reached. I provided two sources of one-to-one teaching which the school could use so that Jason could attend on a part-time basis, the school pieced together further provision, and the local special school offered some time as well. Jason is now attending and formal assessment is underway. The head and the LEA officer have clarified their respective roles and resumed a positive relationship.

REFERENCES

ADLER, R. and ROSS, J. (1955) *Damn Yankees*, New York, Music Theatre Incorporated.

ATWOOD, M. (1988) *Cat's Eye*, London, Virago.

BERG, I., BROWN, I. and HULLIN, R. (1985) *Off School, in Court: an experimental and psychiatric investigation of severe school attendance problems*, New York, Springer-Verlag.

BIRMINGHAM CITY COUNCIL (1991) 'Report of the Chief Education Officer, Education (Special Needs and Welfare Sub-) Committee: 26 November 1991, Exclusions: Statistics for Recent Years', Birmingham, Birmingham City Council.

BLAGG, N. (1987) *School Phobia and its Treatment*, London, Croom Helm.

BLAIR, M. (1991) 'Black pupils and behavioural stereotypes', unpublished paper.

BLYTH, E. and MILNER, J. (1987) 'Non-attendance and the law: the confused role of the social services and education departments' in REID, K. (ed.) *Combating School Absenteeism*, London, Hodder and Stoughton.

BOOTH, T. (1987) 'Sticks and stones: reflections on graffiti at Poundswick School' in BOOTH and COULBY (1987).

BOOTH, T. and COULBY, D. (eds) (1987) *Producing and Reducing Disaffection*, Milton Keynes, Open University Press/The Open University.

BROWN, I., BERG, I., HULLIN, R. (1990) 'Truancy, delinquency and the Leeds adjournment system', *Education and the Law*, 2(1), pp. 47–53.

CARLEN, P., GLEESON, D., WARDHAUGH, J. (1992) *Truancy; the politics of compulsory schooling*, Buckingham, Open University Press.

CASDAGLI, P., GOBY, F. and GRIFFIN, C. (1990) *Only Playing, Miss! the playscript and a workshop approach to the problem of bullying*, Stoke-on-Trent, Trentham Books/PDA.

CENTRAL ADVISORY COUNCIL FOR EDUCATION (ENGLAND) (1963) *Half Our Future*, London, HMSO (the Newsom Report).

CENTRAL ADVISORY COUNCIL FOR EDUCATION (ENGLAND) (1967) *Children and their Primary schools*, London, HMSO (the Plowden Report.

COLE, T. (1986) *Residential Special Education*, Milton Keynes, Open University Press.

COMMISSION FOR RACIAL EQUALITY (CRE) (1983) *Birmingham Local Education Authority and Schools, Referral and Suspension of Pupils, Report of a Formal Investigation*, London, CRE.

COMMISSION FOR RACIAL EQUALITY (CRE) (1988) *Learning in Terror,* London, CRE.

COOPER, P. and UPTON, G. (1990) 'The Elton Report: so what and what next?', *Links*, **16**(1), pp. 19–22.

COOPER, P., UPTON, G. and SMITH, C. (1991) 'Ethnic minority and gender distribution among staff and pupils in facilities for pupils with emotional and behavioural difficulties in England and Wales', *British Journal of Sociology of Education*, **12**(1), pp. 77–94.

CUMMING, C. E., LOWE, T., TULIPS, J. and WAKELING, C. (1981) *Making the Change; a study of the process of the abolition of corporal punishment*, London, Hodder and Stoughton/The Scottish Council for Research in Education.

DAVIES, L. (1984) *Pupil Power: deviance and gender in school*, Lewes, Falmer Press.

DEPARTMENT OF EDUCATION AND SCIENCE (DES) (1989a) *Discipline in schools. Report of the Commission of Enquiry chaired by Lord Elton*, London, HMSO (the Elton Report).

DEPARTMENT OF EDUCATION AND SCIENCE (DES) (1989b) *A Survey of Provision for Pupils with Emotional/Behavioural Difficulties in Maintained Special Schools and Units*, London, HMSO.

DEPARTMENT OF EDUCATION AND SCIENCE (DES) (1991) The Education (Pupils' Attendance Records) Regulations 1991, London, HMSO (Circular 11/91).

DEPARTMENT OF HEALTH AND SOCIAL SECURITY (DHSS) (1968) Report of the Committee on Local Authority and Allied Personnel, London, HMSO (the Seebohm Report).

DRUMMOND COMMUNITY HIGH SCHOOL (1990) *Youth Strategy*, Edinburgh, Drummond Community High School.

EL SAADAWI, N. (1975) *Woman at Point Zero*, London, Zed Books.

FORD, J., MONGON, D. and WHELAN, M. (1982) *Special Education and Social Control*, London, Routledge and Kegan Paul.

GALLOWAY, D. (1985) *Schools and Persistent Absentees*, London, Pergamon.

GILL, D., MAYOR, B. and BLAIR, M. (1992) *Racism and Education; structures and strategies*, London, Sage.

GILLBORN, D. (1990) *'Race', Ethnicity and Education; teaching and learning in multi-ethnic schools*, London, Unwin Hyman.

GORDON, P. (1990) *Racial Violence and Harrassment*, London, Runnymede Trust.

GOODWIN, C. (1983) 'The contribution of support services to integration policy' in BOOTH, T., POTTS, P., (eds) *Integrating Special Education*, Oxford, Blackwell.

GOW, L. and MCPHERSON, A. (1980) *Tell Them from Me*, Aberdeen, Aberdeen University Press.

GRAY, J. and CLOUGH, E. (1984) *Choices at 16, a survey, summary of results*, Sheffield, University of Sheffield.

GRIMSHAW, R. and PRATT, J. (1987) 'Truancy; a case to answer?' in REID, K. (ed.) *Combating School Absenteeism*, London, Hodder and Stoughton.

HARRIS, N. (1989) 'Truancy and legal intervention: in search of the holy grail' *Education and the Law*, **1**(1), pp. 19–26.

HERBERT, C. (1991) *Sexual Harassment in Schools; a guide for teachers*, London, Fulton.

HUMPHRIES, S. (1981) *Hooligans or Rebels? An oral history of working-class childhood and youth 1889–1939*, Oxford, Blackwell.

INNER LONDON EDUCATION AUTHORITY (ILEA) (1987)

JOHNSTONE, M. and MUNN, P. (1987) *Discipline in School; a review of 'causes' and 'cures'*, Edinburgh, Scottish Council for Research in Education.

KELLY, E. (1991) 'Entitlement for all, race, gender and ERA', *Multicultural Teaching*, **10**(1), pp. 17–22.

LANE, D. and TATTUM, D. (eds) (1989) *Bullying in Schools*, Stoke-on-Trent, Trentham Books.

LE RICHE, E. (1988) 'Why do teenage girls truant? A study of school absenteeism in two schools in Merseyside', *Occasional Papers in Sociology and Social Administration No. 8*, London, Roehampton Institute.

LLOYD, G. (ed.) (1992) *Chosen with Care? Responding to disturbing and disruptive behaviour*, Edinburgh, Moray House.

LOCAL GOVERNMENT TRAINING BOARD (1973) *The Role of Training of Education Welfare Officers*, Luton, Local Government Training Board (the Ralphs Report).

LONDON BOROUGH OF LEWISHAM (1991) *Pupil Exclusions from Schools, Summer Term 1990 to Spring Term 1991*, London, London Borough of Lewisham.

LOTHIAN REGIONAL COUNCIL (1991) 'Joint Sub-Committee on Integration and Youth Strategy Pupils Excluded from School: sessions 1989/90 and 1990/91', Lothian Regional Council, Edinburgh.

LOTHIAN REGIONAL COUNCIL (1992) *Youth Strategy: guidelines for school liaison groups*, Edinburgh, Lothian Regional Council.

MACDONALD, I., BHAVNANI, R., KHAN, L. and JOHN, G. (1989) *Murder in the playground: the report of the Macdonald inquiry into racism and racial violence in Manchester schools*, London, Longsight Press.

MAINES, B. and ROBINSON, G. (1991) 'Don't beat the bullies', *Educational Psychology in Practice*, **7**(3) pp. 168–72.

MELLOR, A. (1990) 'Bullying in Scottish secondary schools, *Spotlights 23*, Edinburgh, Scottish Council for Research in Education.

NATIONAL UNION OF TEACHERS (NUT) (1992) *Union Survey Reveals Jump in Pupil Exclusions*, London, NUT (press release).

NEWELL, P. (1989) *Children Are People Too: the case against physical punishment*, London, Bedford Square Press.

NOTTINGHAMSHIRE COUNTY COUNCIL (1991) *Pupil Exclusions from Nottingham Secondary Schools*, Nottingham, Nottinghamshire County Council.

OLWEUS, D. (1989) 'Bully/victim problems among schoolchildren: basic facts and effects of a school-based intervention program' in RUBIN, K. and PEPLER, D. (eds) *The Development and Treatment of Childhood Aggression*, Hillsdale (NJ), Lawrence Erlbaum Associates.

THE OPEN UNIVERSITY (1992) *ED536 Race, Education and Society*, Milton Keynes, The Open University.

PATERSON, F. (1989) *Out of Place: public policy and the emergence of truancy*, Lewes, Falmer Press.

PEARSON, G. (1983) *Hooligan. A history of respectable fears*, Basingstoke, Macmillan Education Ltd.

PIKAS, A. (1989) 'The common concern method for the treatment of mobbing' in ROLAND, E. and MUNTHE, E. (eds) *Bullying, an International Perspective*, London, Fulton.

POOLE, K. (1987) *Education Law*, London, Sweet and Maxwell.

REID, K. (1987) 'Combating School Absenteeism; main conclusions' in REID, K. (ed.) *Combating School Absenteeism*, London, Hodder and Stoughton.

SASSOON, D. (1992) 'The exclusion of pupils: is it the most appropriate way of dealing with indiscipline?' *Education and the Law*, **4**(2) pp. 55–9.

SCHOSTAK, J. (1983) *Maladjusted Schooling: deviance, social control and individuality in secondary schooling*, Lewes, Falmer Press.

SCOTTISH EDUCATION DEPARTMENT (SED) (1966) 'Appendix to Liaison Committee on Educational Matters, Report by Sub-Committee on the Elimination of Corporal Punishment in Schools, LA(66)1', Edinburgh, SED.

SCOTTISH EDUCATION DEPARTMENT (SED) (1977) *Truancy and Indiscipline in Schools in Scotland*, Edinburgh, HMSO (the Pack Report).

SCOTTISH OFFICE EDUCATION DEPARTMENT (SOED) (1990) *Choosing with Care: provision for pupils with behavioural, emotional and social difficulties. A report of Her Majesty's Inspectorate*, Edinburgh, HMSO.

SHAW, G. B. (1921) *Parents and Children in Misalliance*, Paris, Bernhard Tauchnitz.

SIMON, B. (1991) *Education and the Social Order 1940–1990*, London, Lawrence and Wishart.

SKINNER, A. (1992) *Bullying; an annotated bibliography of literature and resources*, Leicester, Youth Work Press.

SMITH, P. (1991) 'The silent nightmare: bullying and victimisation in school peer groups', *The Psychologist*, **14**(6) pp. 243–8.

STIRLING, M. (1992) 'The Education Reform Act and EBD Children', *Young Minds Newsletter No. 10*, (the National Association for Child and Family Mental Health), March, pp. 8–9.

TABOR, M.C. (1891) in BOOTH, C. (ed.) *Labour and Life of the People*, Vol. 2, London, Williams and Northgate.

TATTUM, D. and HERBERT, G. (1990) *Bullying: a positive response*, Cardiff, CIHE.

TOMLINSON, S. (1982) *A Sociology of Special Education*, London, Routledge and Kegan Paul.

TOPPIN, N. (1987) 'School assessment panels at St Augustine's School' in BOOTH, T. and COULBY, D. (eds) *Producing and Reducing Disaffection*, Milton Keynes, Open University Press/The Open University.

TYERMAN, M. (1968) *Truancy*, London, University of London Press.

WARDHAUGH, J. (1990) 'Regulating truancy; the role of the education welfare service', *The Sociological Review*, **38**(4) pp. 735–64.

WRIGHT, C. (1987) ' "The English culture is being swamped": racism in secondary schools' in BOOTH and COULBY (1987).

ACKNOWLEDGEMENTS

Grateful acknowledgement is made to the following for permission to reproduce material in these units:

Text

Richard Adler and Jerry Ross, 'A little brains, a little talent', from *Damn Yankees*, reproduced by permission of Warner Chappell Music Ltd.

Figure

Figure 2: Munro, N., 'Discipline without the belt', *The Times Educational Supplement*, 20 August 1982, © Times Newspapers Ltd 1982.

Illustrations

Page 68: (*lower cartoon*): the Editor, *Education*, published by Longman Group UK Ltd; (*top left, middle left*): Ralph Steadman; (*top right, middle centre, middle right*): David McKee.

E242: UNIT TITLES